THE
ALTMAN
CLOSE

PREVIOUS WORKS

It's Your Move

JOSH ALTMAN

**MILLION-DOLLAR
NEGOTIATION
TACTICS**
FROM
**AMERICA'S TOP
REAL ESTATE AGENT**

THE
ALTMAN
CLOSE

WILEY

For general information on our other products and services or for technical support, please contact
our Customer Care Department within the United States at (800) 762-2974, outside the United
States at (317) 572-3993 or fax (317) 572-4002.

Wiley publishes in a variety of print and electronic formats and by print-on-demand. Some material
included with standard print versions of this book may not be included in e-books or in print-on-
demand. If this book refers to media such as a CD or DVD that is not included in the version you
purchased, you may download this material at http://booksupport.wiley.com. For more information
about Wiley products, visit www.wiley.com.

Library of Congress Cataloging-in-Publication Data

Names: Altman, Josh, 1979- author.
Title: The Altman close : million-dollar negotiation tactics from America's
    top real estate agent / Josh Altman.
Description: Hoboken, New Jersey : John Wiley & Sons, Inc., 2019. | Includes
    index. |
Identifiers: LCCN 2018061434 (print) | LCCN 2019003660 (ebook) | ISBN
    9781119560104 (ePDF) | ISBN 9781119560128 (ePub) | ISBN 9781119560111
    (hardcover)
Subjects: LCSH: Success in business. | Selling. | Negotiation. | Real estate
    business.
Classification: LCC HF5386 (ebook) | LCC HF5386 .A5439 2019 (print) | DDC
    333.33068/8—dc23
LC record available at https://lccn.loc.gov/2018061434

Printed in the United States of America

V10008469   022719

To my amazing wife Heather. The greatest close of all. Your support in the Altman Brothers office, our home, and life, has allowed me to consistently operate at the top of my game and be the best closer I can be. You're an incredible mom and have given me the best gift ever . . . our daughter Lexi. I look forward to many more negotiations with you in life. You are definitely the toughest negotiator I know, and you always keep me on my toes. You're my Ace.

CONTENTS

Foreword   Robert Herjavec, Shark Tank   *xi*
Preface: Pre-Game Pep Talk   *xiii*

Part I   Prep Through Open   1
Chapter 1   Game-Time Mentality   3
Chapter 2   The Players, the Field, the Shot Clock   9
Chapter 3   My First Close   19
Chapter 4   All In with LA Real Estate and BRAVO TV   23
                 Negotiating Is All   24
                 Going Hollywood, TV Time   25
Chapter 5   Rules of the Game: First Impressions   31
                 Impressions Matter   32
                 10 Rules to Make a Positive First Impression   35
Chapter 6   The Dream Team: You Can't Do It Alone   39
Chapter 7   Fresh Eyes on the Prize   45
Chapter 8   All About the Open   51
                 Know More than the 'Hood   52
                 Watch Your Back   55
                 Networking and Giving to Get   56
Chapter 9   Open Houses for Clients, Brokers, and Insiders   59
                 Don't Tour, Sell   59
                 Broker's Opens   61
                 Insider Opens and Strategic Alliances   62
Chapter 10   Create an In-Your-Face Brand, 24/7   65
                 Working the Web: Social Media and the Press   66
                 Give Expert Advice   68
                 Concierge Extraordinaire   70

Chapter 11   Golden Hammers and 20 Questions for Sellers   73
              Shut Up and Listen   73
              The Altman 20 (Questions for Sellers)   76
Chapter 12   Size Up the Property: Pricing and Timing   81
              Reading the Property: Questions I Ask Myself   82
              Let's Talk Pricing   84
Chapter 13   Close the Open on Sellers: Talk Marketing, then Sign 89
Chapter 14   Close the Open on Buyers: The Altman 12   93
Chapter 15   Off to Work: Take a Breath First   99

Part II   The Work   101
Chapter 16   Working with Buyers: Part Chemistry, Part Therapy   103
              Assessing Personality Types   104
              Analyzing the Buyer   105
              Calming the Buyer's Fears   106
Chapter 17   Strategizing with Sellers: Getting Ready for War   109
              The Battle Plan   109
              Managing the Troops   111
Chapter 18   Weapons: Listing Language, Interior Design, and Staging 113
              A Killer Description   113
              Killer Design   115
              Staging for Battle   116
Chapter 19   The Killer Combo: Drone and 360° Photos Plus Staging 119
Chapter 20   On the Battlefield: More on Open Houses and
              Broker's Opens   125
              Who to Invite?   127
              Work the Party   128
              What About Neighbor(hood)s?   129
              Sell Strong Points and Knowledge   130
Chapter 21   Price Drops Are Not Always Downers   133
Chapter 22   Go Win the War   139

Part III   The Close   141

Chapter 23   Making an Offer   143
             Settling on the Price   144
             Inspections and Contingencies   149
             More Deal Sweetener Details   152
             As for Curve Balls: Play by Your Rules and Get the House   154

Chapter 24   Getting an Offer   157

Chapter 25   Multiple and Counteroffers   161
             Negotiating on the Clock   162
             No Rules? Use Hammers for Leverage   165

Chapter 26   Psyching Out Business Styles   171

Chapter 27   Putting on the Poker Face   177
             The Anger Hammer   177
             Know the Classic Hard-Baller Moves   182
             Use Confidence to Grab the Hammer   184

Chapter 28   The Walk-Away   187
             How to Walk Away   190

Chapter 29   Be a Shark: Eat, Swim, Devour   193

Part IV   Plays from the Book   195

Chapter 30   Play #1: Damn, the Studio Head's Pissed   197

Chapter 31   Play #2: Three Clients, One Property   199

Chapter 32   Play #3: The Middle Men Kings   201

Chapter 33   Play #4: The Most Expensive Garage Ever Sold   203

Chapter 34   Play #5: The Paramedics of Real Estate   207

Chapter 35   The Final Play: Confession   209

Acknowledgments   213
About the Author   215
Index   217

FOREWORD
by Robert Herjavec, *Shark Tank*

I first met Josh Altman five years ago when I was perusing properties online. I saw what I now know to be synonymous with his name: a great piece of real estate. Josh represented the house of interest and I emailed his general website immediately. Within minutes, he personally responded. The man already had options for me. He had a plan. Not only was he ready to show me the house that caught my attention, but he had lined up a few other exclusives as well, properties that were off-market and unknown to the public.

From our brief exchange over mere email, I knew I respected Altman for a few standout reasons. In my life as a businessman who deals with other professionals daily, even judging them on television's *Shark Tank*, there are certain traits that make few entrepreneurs rise above the rest. Communication, creative outside-of-the-box thinking, hustle, and personalized attentiveness to clients always prevail. In my line of work these attributes are imperative. I knew at once, Josh had them in spades.

Within weeks, Josh showed me a couple dozen properties. One in particular stood out, but as I had been working with a few other realtors prior, I ended up purchasing a house that someone else showed me before The Altman Brothers came into the scene. That's usually where the story ends for most people. Not for Josh.

Three years down the line, I had listed the house I bought with the realtor who sold it to me, only he could not find a buyer. It had been six months on the market with no bites. In the meantime, Josh had been consistently reaching out to me every few months. His follow-up was always consistent. The day came when I needed a change from my current realtor and the choice was a no-brainer. I gave Josh a shot at listing the home and as if effortless, he sold it. Not only did he sell it, he knocked it out of the park when it came to negotiating and closing the buyer. He treated my money like it was his own and was extremely strategic in the negotiations. I remember specifically when it got to a certain price, he insisted with the confidence of the expert he is. "Robert," he said, "take the deal!"

I trusted him. I listened. I signed. The man was right. It was an excellent deal for me.

While in escrow closing on that house, I tasked Josh with finding me a new home. Little did I know, he had remembered everything I liked and disliked from our first encounter three years prior. He tracked down the specific house I had adored and approached the owner. Turns out they wanted to sell. The fact that Josh remembered a preferred house from three years earlier showed me what kind of listener he is. In a customer service business, listening to your clients' needs is so important, and it separates the good businessmen from the great. I was impressed and my wife and I were ecstatic to have the chance to own a house we loved. We bought it and live there today.

From that moment on, I told Josh he was my realtor for life. Still to this day, whenever I call, email, or text him, Josh always answers, ready and prepared to get the information I need. I get pitched business ideas from entrepreneurs all the time on *Shark Tank*, but rarely do I see someone who can negotiate and close deals like Josh Altman. Now, when I think real estate, I think of Josh Altman and The Altman Close.

PREFACE: PRE-GAME PEP TALK

Let's get right to it. This book is more than real estate. This book is Hollywood. By that I mean I am Hollywood. YOU have the capability and potential of being Hollywood, too. I use "Hollywood" not in the pretentious, superficial, glitz-and-glamour sense of the phrase – take it from a blue-collar Boston guy who worked in the mailroom – and not as a geographical location. "Hollywood" in Altman-speak is making the biggest deals at the highest levels with the wealthiest and most financially successful entrepreneurs, success not just being measured by bank accounts.

We'll cover that, but to start, this book is about closing, something I do over 180 times per year at record profits. Check my stats. Hell, check the *Wall Street Journal*. You'll find me. Closing is about opening, which together is serving your client with the upmost respect, servicing your community, and yes, making money, lots of it. I don't care if you're in London, Dubai, Iowa, or Arkansas. You have the opportunity to make your business, your brand, and yourself "Hollywood." This is a mentality, a physicality, and a reality. The Altman Brothers don't dance. We make money moves, and you can dance to that.

From the moment I wake up ready for battle – gym to shower to embroidered suit – I am closing a deal. Whether on the street, in a Beverly Hills mansion, or on the sports field, the ball is in my hands; the clock is counting down, 3-2-1. This is what I have prepared for, the way I've set it up from the first play, the way I've adapted, overcoming any obstacle thrown my way. It's all up to me to be a champion. It's up to me to close, the exact way I've planned all along, each path different. If you don't want the ball in your hands, if the pressure doesn't excite you, then just put this book down and read my previous literary work, *It's Your Move*.

This book goes beyond that one. This is the advanced course. This is the vision-board pinned with a check written to your mother, seven zeros minimum to offer because you and your kids are already covered. I cannot give you the drive, the work ethic, the passion, but I can kick you in the ass as my college football coach did to me. I can be straight A-to-B, no nonsense, and relay to you the tools it takes to be a feared beast – a shark. I'm Josh Altman. What's going on? Let me tell you how I can help you today. Translation: I know how to help us both. You'll want this.

I have the respect and the knowledge to give you the necessary respect and knowledge. Only you can be accountable for you and your success. This business is on your shoulders alone. Do you have what it takes to listen, to dig deep, come off the bench and Tom Brady this? Can you be the GOAT (greatest-of-all-time) in this? Do you have the thick skin to win, to lose, and to use that experience to come out on top in the big game, time and time again? If so, turn the page. Step on the field and know that the one goal, no matter what it takes to get there, is to score and score big, with continuous victories, one stacked on top of the other. We don't have time for anything else. The clock doesn't wait. I thank you in advance for your precious seconds. Now let's not waste them. Let me teach you how to thank yourself.

Success: You want this or not? How bad do you want it? Are you willing to sacrifice? Are you willing to be cutthroat? If you think that "cutthroat" means to screw someone over, then please keep reading for your own sake. That is not success. That does not get repeat calls.

In today's world of misconstrued controversy, success is dignity for yourself and others. Business is business, and for some that can be extremely personal. Closing real estate deals affects people's lives on many levels. Small fish or big dog, the principle remains the same: You will not make everyone happy all of the time, but if you honor yourself, if you honor your client, if you honor your community, if you honor your competitors no matter your true opinion of them, then you can win for all, time and time again, each victory more in your favor.

Compromise makes a relationship, and cutthroat compromise can be your best friend. It may not always be your ideal outcome, but a friend nonetheless, one that returns, the give-and-take, a friend that honors in value.

We all love a slam dunk, a Hail Mary caught, a grand slam, yet even in this past year, when my second-home team the Los Angeles Dodgers lost the World Series to my beloved Boston Red Sox, the Dodgers took out a full-page ad in the *Boston Globe* congratulating the Sox on their win. That's class. That makes a loss a win for them – a form of close in itself.

If you think I just dated this technique of closing by invoking killing for kindness and the Golden Rule, then pause to acknowledge this: We all live in the moment because others lived in the past with a hopeful vision of the future. We are that future. That said: This book is Hollywood. Now let's get you the gold statue no matter what happened before, as long as you own it, remember it, and learn from it. Let's get you the win. Let's get you paid. Let's close!

Are you ready for what you say you want? Are you prepared to learn? Success: How bad do you need it? How much do you need it for everyone? How much do you need it for yourself? I have built a real estate empire. I have built success by constructing fear in others with my aggressive attitude toward business. They call me "The Shark" for a reason. Now, I open you to the embrace. Let's begin to be better. Let's be the best – the GOAT. Let's all win – with the Altman Close.

Part I

PREP THROUGH OPEN

Chapter 1

GAME-TIME MENTALITY

Before we get to the numbers, and before we get to me, here's the thing. The most important rule in life is to show up and show up on time. By on time I mean early. By early, I mean ahead of schedule, prepared, in warrior mindset, questions asked and answered in all ways, ready to go. The clock started yesterday.

If you're late to bed, you're late to wake up, maybe not physically, but definitely mentally. If you're late to breakfast, your morning routine, then you're already chasing. If you're late to the locker room, you're late to what you should have been able to bring to the table. Even worse, you've now missed the coach's plan. You're late for the game. You don't deserve to be on the court. You're not a player. You're not ready to close. Don't be late to yourself.

The beauty and the common attraction of the real estate business is the idea of freedom, that you are your own boss, the coach. Wait – cut that thought out right now. If you want to be your own boss, then you'll understand and respect the fact that your client is the boss, the coach, no matter how you feel about them personally, no matter the situation.

There's no excuse to be late – not car trouble, family emergencies, whatever. Yes, things happen, but you can bet your ass that in most cases your new client has a family too, and there they are, ready to strategize, ready to play, ready to attack. They're not late because they are showing up for their family, setting them up in the best seats, the best arena. They care about that family. Do you? You'd better.

If they have no family, then there's even less leeway for being late. They are there for themselves, racing the clock to build whatever is important to them. They have a game plan and they have drafted you to be on their team. If you're not punctual, if you're not there with guns blazing, uniform on, and a positive attitude ready to play, then you already don't deserve to be on the team. Let me say this again, if you truly want to be your own boss, know that your client is the boss.

Like it or not, we are all human. We all have an ego. We all want to be a baller in whatever sense the word works for us. In our case, it usually means getting the best deal. As soon as you show your current boss a flaw in your preparation, in your ability to work with them and take direction, a lack of confidence, cockiness, or ego, you have compromised your role on the team. You're late. You're wrong. You're done.

You don't take them seriously so why should they want you. You've created doubt in a business they are already uncomfortable with, even if seasoned. Like the reputations of nickel-and-diming construction workers or mechanics, of lying lawyers, slippery entertainment agents, and greasy car salesman, a long line of unreliable jerks have tainted our reputations as real estate agents.

So you begin against the odds, not trusted, a possible scumbag out only for yourself ready to rip someone off. Your new coach knows this and yet has gambled on you. Their reputation, career, money, safety of their children, getting laid that night by their lover, all of it, depends on the faith they have put in you. And let me tell you, the sharks, the big dogs, the ones with the loot you want to put in *your* pocket, will have no tolerance for you. There are plenty of players to pick from. The good ones are ready and beyond.

Believe me, your clients are just itching to fire your ass, to flex their muscles and reassure themselves that they are in charge. They want to feel better about themselves and not view themselves as weak, as suckers – or they simply know the ropes and don't tolerate bullshit. They expect top-grade. They are ballers who don't have time for nonsense. Waiver – and forget about it.

You see me on television, *Million Dollar Listing: Los Angeles*. Yes, it's a reality show. Cast members throw glasses of wine at each other and do other petty shit. But the real business is the real estate, the properties, the deals, the clients, and the closings. All very real: I did 189 closings last year.

You see ten of those on the show. How many times have you seen me roll into a meeting that starts off with a threat to my job? Ten. "I want it this way, Josh. I want it that way, Altman. Get it done or I'll find someone else!" I am proud to say, and my stats have proven, that many of those same clients – my coaches – end the episodes on television and in actual life saying, "I can't believe you pulled that off," grinning ear-to-ear, the cigar lit, ready to do business again.

So you're there, but are you there mentally prepared? From the moment I wake up, as I do my morning stretch, drink my protein shake, slip on my sharp-as-hell uniform, kiss my beautiful wife, hug my daughter, and pull out of my driveway, in the car of my dreams, away from the house I always wanted. I am closing. I am a beast! I am ready for battle, ready to win, ready to close, to open, to work, to make everyone money. I want my boss to know that when it comes down to the last-second huddle, his most trusted and reliable option is to coordinate the play so I get the ball.

Can I stroll in and still maybe win the game on charm, luck, skill, and an easy challenge? Sure. But that's not good enough. At this level – the Altman "Hollywood" level – my job is to win to do it in spectacular fashion against all odds. I want my coach, in the postgame interview in front of all the cameras, to brag that I made his job easier. Choosing me as his superstar makes him look like a beautiful genius but my stock goes up.

Then I have to do it again. It's expected. I have to meet that demand and surpass it. In another postgame interview my coach, again wowed by my lead to victory, laughs in amazement. Now, every team wants me and mine will fight, sacrifice, and pay to keep me on their team.

The beauty of real estate is that there's no limit to the amount of teams we can win championship rings for. Don't try it. Do it. If you blow it, get up and do it again. Prove yourself even against adversity. Those hard times will happen, but coach is counting on you. *You* are counting on you. Be prepared. Become your own coach by allowing all to be one.

My empire reigns from Hollywood in the traditional sense of the term as much as it does the Altman sense, so let me reference one of my favorite classic films. Have you ever seen Martin Scorcese's *Casino* starring Robert De Niro? If you haven't, eat some antacids and watch it.

In this movie based on a true-life scenario, De Niro plays a sports bookie who sets the point-spread lines for every game – the coach of his crew. As any great boss, he relies on preparation and knowledge. In return, he is able to assess the most predictable outcome of each sporting event, making even the gamblers, the suckers, feel like they are the coaches. He gives them the knowledge to make them think they will win while guaranteeing himself and his employers – in this case the mafia (and you may want to steer clear of them) – that he will win, for them and for all.

In the movie (and in real life too) the mafia bosses gave the bookie, called Sam "Ace" Rothstein in the film, the keys to a Vegas casino. True story. What did Rothstein know beyond any average guy picking up the sports page? The answer is personal information, insider knowledge. Is today's freezing wind chill a factor for an opposing team used to warmer weather on their home field ? Did the point guard's dog just die? The quarterback spent the weekend in drunken tears after finding out his girlfriend was cheating on him. How's he feeling today? The basketball court has a soft spot on the baseline, which can deaden the spring in an athlete's step, and the rim is tilted a degree to the left, which can change the ball's trajectory. Who does that effect and how? It's the same in real estate.

A few years ago, I had a premiere property in the 90210 – Beverly Hills. The lot was baller, but the clients/coaches were an emotional mess. I'm talking two siblings who were fighting over their childhood home that they couldn't afford to keep. The brother wanted to sell. The sister wouldn't go for it. It was tense. What was my job? To give the brother the best tools and arguments to convince his sister to sell, the offer no one could refuse. I needed to provide every option. To do this right I had to show up and show up on time, prepared, ready to please, ready to close from the open. I needed to be "Hollywood."

A great real estate agent must act as architect, interior designer, contractor, city planner, legal consultant, insurance agent, salesman, dream maker, fortune teller, and most of all, therapist. I had done my research. I knew the neighborhood comps. I knew the insurance zones. I knew the local ordinances. I knew the community, the school zones, the crime rate and the walking distance to shops. I knew the nearby sports bar where the brother suggested we first meet. I knew the prices of necessary renovations and I had the eye for suggestions they never considered on how to beautify the home. I had paid attention to all of this with closing in mind, as any real estate agent worth their salt should have done.

But there was one more problem. The sister loved the old oak, the very tree she'd climb in childhood, the tree where she and her brother had their names carved in the trunk. She'd never let the tree be uprooted from her childhood memories or from her now-adult, eco-friendly heart. She'd rather have the house burn down. I can't tell you how many times I've met sellers who exclaim, "But I don't want anyone to change the style of the house, no knockdowns, and they definitely can't remove that special tree." It's an unreasonable ball-bust, but we humans are ball-busters, and we often want to preserve and share what is special to us. It's our nature.

So, how'd I learn about the tree? What I'm about to say is one of the most overlooked elements in our business along with a general simple rule of life – I asked the guy! Then I listened. I repeat. I asked and listened. I could have asked the basic questions any real estate agent would ask, but I needed to be great, the greatest of all time. I needed to be more than a real estate agent. I needed to be a friend. I knew going in that this property was only for sale due to a death in the family and the remaining siblings were at odds about what to do. I needed to be a person who cared and who helped. In return, this would also help me; it would be good for the soul, the head, the heart, and ultimately the pocket. As my wonderful parents had taught me, this mentality was bigger than the close – it was life, my clients' life *and* mine.

It was my moment to shine, to fix the problem, to make the sale, to close. I showed on time, prepared, and asked this grieving soul the details, the little personal stuff. Not only did this express my comforting interest in him and his family, but it led me toward an end zone he never considered when wondering how to achieve the same goal and then sell it to his sister against her opposition. I needed to have ready options for any posed scenario. He needed options to take back to his sister, who was a kind of boss to him. It was my job to give him these valuable options with value assessed. I pleased my coach. I came to close through opening – offering new solutions he could pitch to his sister and help her realize a reasonable price, something she never thought could be done and never wanted to confront.

We are human. We're sensitive. Respect this. It takes time to sort out emotions and heal, especially after the loss of a loved one. By showing up on time, prepared to ask carefully crafted, pertinent questions, I allowed the family to fast-track the time it would have taken for them to reach their breaking point – the "ah, screw it" moment: "I just can't do it anymore." Allowing a client to reach that point is something you can't always control, but it is my job to make the best effort to let people see the true story, to give them the keys to their casino. I'm not just selling homes; I'm helping people close their hardships. In return, I make a better deal for each of us, a better day – a win for all. That's being prepared. That is "Game-Time Mentality."

In the end, the sister couldn't disagree with the circumstances and I made her feel a lot better about the inevitable. She gave up the tree and she gave up the house. When the next contractor was removing the tree, I made sure to preserve small pieces of the trunk where the brother and sister had carved their names. I sent those pieces framed and glassed to each of them, a personal sentimental touch. We're not only friends now, but they've sent me a dozen more coaches all over the nation who still have me as their starting superstar. I showed up and showed up on time, prepared for the game, and everyone won. I pleased my coach, my boss, and me.

"Game Time" in Altman "Hollywood" means showing up on time, prepared and ready, in your heart as well as your head. If you don't understand that, then you'll never be on my team or be able to compete against it.

Now let's fast forward. Let's get to some rock-star living. Let's get to the Altman Brothers, modern-day Los Angeles, 2019.

Chapter 2

THE PLAYERS, THE FIELD, THE SHOT CLOCK

Who am I? My name is Josh "the Shark" Altman, aka "the Rain Man of Real Estate," of the Los Angeles–based Altman Brothers Team. As you read this book you'll notice that sometimes I lead a chapter with my stats to instill confidence in my clients. Please allow me to do so now.

Last year, out of 2.5 million agents, the *Wall Street Journal* ranked me #22 and the #1 team in Los Angeles all while filming a TV show for 10 months, writing my last best-selling book, filming a Youtube Channel, recording a podcast, flipping houses, doing 30 keynote speeches around the world, and mentoring thousands of real estate agents. Oh yeah, and having a baby. I have closed over $3 billion in sales. Currently, I have 58 listings with over $100 million in escrow at all times. As my bio reads:

Altman's reputation precedes him with various record-breaking sales and listings, including a $145 million listing in Beverly Hills, the most expensive one-bedroom ever sold at $21,500,000, the priciest lease in the history of Beverly Hills, the costliest condo sale in Santa Monica, and the highest-price-per-square-foot home sold in the Hollywood Hills. He once approached a big shot studio head one morning at a local gym and sold his house – which wasn't on the market – for $11.25 million by close of day.

There, now you know, but that's enough about me. Let's talk about the game.

Buying and selling real estate is about time, the shot clock. Our market is the world, but our home field is Los Angeles, the city that made us local globalists. This place is crazy. You've never seen anything like it. For my brother Matt and me – moving to LA and setting up in Beverly Hills – it was like we were bank robbers in the Wild West, with every money-train there for the taking.

For East Coast guys like us, hustlers with the service mentality, this town gets your adrenaline pumping for more than fame and fortune – it's the thrill of the deal that keeps us going. Hell no. It's the hunt, the catch, and no release. The biggest whales from all over the world, they all want a piece, and we want to sell it to them.

I'm talking luxury real estate. I'm talking $20 million-plus mega-mansions under construction, pulling our humble $12 million villas upward because houses are literally judged by the company they keep. Try being a property-flipper on the Westside dealing with a real estate agent who doesn't understand Altman "Hollywood," the shot clock, or "Game Time." If a launch is stalled, if a property goes stale, which will happen here even prior to listing, your coach/client is getting smacked with $20,000 to $40,000 monthly carrying costs: pennies to few, but not to a businessperson who's been around the block. This dirt piles up and it buries you quick.

The seller's market here is fierce, bloodthirsty. Many of my clients won't even look at a property if it was shown to the general public. They want privacy, exclusivity, something no one else can have or has even seen before.

These are the movie stars, hip-hop moguls, fashion models, television producers, professional athletes, kings of property development, the tech industry, hotel heiresses, socialites, and all of their high-end attorneys and doctors who make their homes in the Hollywood Hills, Bel Air, Santa Monica, Marina del Rey, Brentwood, Pacific Palisades, Malibu, Beverly Hills.

This is the clientele who demand to see and sell via pocket listings – the "exclusives" that never make it to the MLS. Pocket listings take more time and energy because showing and selling them is a one-on-one process. But Matt and I have the reach within this top-dollar community to fulfill the need with buyers who want to play ball.

Also, some of our clients are developers who buy properties the way everybody else shops for new sneakers. For many of our clients, a real-estate deal won't make or break their whole bank. This is West Los Angeles. Private jets are common transportation. We kill it here.

But beyond the Hollywood Hills are my sweet spots, the $2- to $4-million deals that power my business day in and day out. The clock runs differently there: a week on the market and a listing starts to go cold and cramp up; a month passes and you can forget about multiple offers. You have to beat that clock. Do it and you make money, if not, you have to drop the price. You'll have to reinvent the listing.

If your re-launch isn't on point, just take the property off the field in a stretcher, light a match, whatever. It's done. I'll tell you soon how we nurse it back to health. We're great at that, reviving the deal. To dying properties, the Altman Brothers are the best doctors around.

Don't take my word for it. Matt and I did $423 million in sales last year. I'm aware of what we're up against. You see, any savvy real estate agent or home shopper can figure out on the MLS how many times and for how long a house has been listed. Hell, just Google it. It'll tell you.

Buyers are sure to think there's something wrong with the house and they'll want out, as if touching the place would hurt their image, their brand, their team. In a town where you're only as good as your last project no one picks up a dying horse, they just cover it in a tarp on the track, put it down right in front of the crowd.

Study after study has backed this. The longer a house is for sale, the less likely it will get asking price. In and around LA, this clock ticks faster than anywhere in the world. A listing's life expectancy is short. Taxes, loans and mortgage rates are high. Act fast, you'll make money. Ignore this, you'll lose money.

When money's lost, the locals get restless, the word gets out and you have to know how to hold on to your successful image *and* keep the jackals at bay. The only way to do that is to make bank and keep your eye on the shot clock. Balancing urgency, strategy, and patience is a delicate game. It requires finesse. It requires the Altman Close.

Matt and I were working on a sale in the Hollywood Hills, a glorious Italianate celebrity compound on a cul de sac hovering above hawks in the clouds over LA. A builder bought it, intending to renovate and resell; he installed Carrera-marbled hallways, vine-covered pergolas, hand-forged iron railings, and a series of outdoor decks with fireplaces for entertaining. What he did was beautiful.

We proposed a listing figure. He thought it was worth more than what we suggested. He hired some other agent. The guy then bumped around, struggling to sell it at a higher price with that other agent. The nerve, but hey, we know the drill. It happens. Everyone wants to be a baller until they get stuck with the ball.

After some time with his face in the dirt and his pockets getting plucked, he finally came back to us ready to accept our suggestion, the one we'd given him in the first place six months earlier. After being on the market for six months, this house should have been a pig.. But it's LA, man. You never know. The old agent couldn't sell the house because of all the construction around it. That was a major issue for him in showing the property to his clients. The trick is to be aware, to be ahead, to think the way hockey legend Wayne Gretzky's father taught him: "Don't go to where the puck is, go to where it's going to be." You have to be quick, ready to adjust, adapt, and overcome.

The surrounding homes that were being constructed brought this listing back to life. The new-construction houses surrounding it came in at an average of 15,000 to 20,000 square feet per property. Those are big houses. Our listing was about 11,000 square feet, a rare home that is actually scaled to human beings, designed for indoor-outdoor Southern California living and now the smallest mansion on an exclusive mega-mansion hill, home to the 1% of the 1%. We eventually sold the house. Instead of letting the construction work against us, we used it as a positive and embraced it, using it in our pitch as the most affordable deal on an A+block. We sold it for future value, not what it's worth now. We went where the puck was going to be.

Some may say we got lucky with that one, but there are always the signs. You either see them or you don't. In our business, if you don't, yep, you lose money. We make money. We close. That's why our phone rings.

What did we do differently than others? We sold it, not just listed it: two very different things, which we'll talk about later. We didn't quit. Almost 99% of the time, a deal is within reach if all parties stay engaged. Quit, and you've taken yourself out of the game. Why are we successful, why do we close? We know this. We're aware. We're on point. We move and we move fast.

Beyond LA, the current average time for a house sale is 70 days according to Redfin.com, or 65 days according to realtor.com, but it doesn't matter. You're already behind the clock if you care about those numbers. We don't use those stats as our benchmark. We beat them and as a result . . . say it with me . . . we make money.

Either way, LA or not, the turnaround to close varies wildly from market to market, economic cycle to cycle, season to season. Houses sell more quickly and closer to list in school-time months.. Six months on the market – the length of a standard listing agreement – is time enough to sell most houses if you know the Altman Close.

It sounds more simple than it is, most challenges do, but I can assure you, selling real estate on a high-end level will either get you right up in the morning or keep you down for good. Many who take a few uppercuts to the chin never get off the stool and go back in the ring. So, we've perfected a system, a well-oiled machine. Game time.

1. Have an effective strategy. Show up and show up on time, prepared.
2. Execute it without time-costing errors. It's A-B-C. You move down the alphabet too fast, or skip a letter, you'll have to backtrack. Then you owe instead of earn.
3. Don't quit. Throw in the towel and you may not get that second chance. Ever.

From Step 1 to Step 3, this all culminates with the close in mind. We like our clients, our coaches, to have the same mindset. We like athletes.

Matt and I were athletes. (You may not know it, but I kicked field goals for Syracuse during the Donovan McNabb quarterback years. Matt kicked for the football team of University of Colorado.) We respect discipline, hardship, pressure, and anyone who fights through adversity. It's the same in real estate. As soon as we sign the listing we know the shot clock is counting down and we're off. We don't stop. No time for error. No time for tears. We close.

As I said earlier, I can't teach you Step 3. That's in you. I can lift your spirits. I can give you constructive criticism. I can shame the hell out of you. But that's not my job in this book. My job is to teach you how to close from the door, the way I close, on point, successful, fast, like a shark.

As for Steps 1 and 2, I am going to show you how I leverage time to close deals by biting right through them – breakfast, lunch, and dinner. I'm wild hungry and you should be too if you want to take a listing from me or from my world. Here are a couple of meaty buzzwords for you to chew on, or call them utensils to facilitate your deals:

– Exclusivity
– Inventory
– Pricing

If you create a sense of urgency, you close. If someone wants the property at a certain price you like, you close. If more than one person wants the spot, you get the best offer and you close. If someone wants it for another price, you work it out, and you close. If you don't like any of the offers, and you have the confidence to bounce, blow them off in a respectful manner and keep working. I consider myself a hustler and I'm damn proud of it.

In fact, this book is a hustle, but a straight-up honest one, as are all my deals, and it's just the hustle you need. I'm here to make a deal, to cash a check. If I don't, I've just burned a lot of time. So, I don't burn time. I make money. You want to be a great agent, go where the money is while keeping the others buzzing along. Swallow them next.

It's not an opinion for me to state that after many years of buying and selling in this market, the Altman Brothers team has turned our real estate business into a monster. Our listings, aka "product launches," are constant and creative. We use time to elicit offers and create counteroffer competition.

Still, there's always the unexpected. In a flash, you have to adjust, adapt, and overcome. Do so and you make money. The bank seizes the property, figure it out. An earthquake hits, figure it out. The seller stabs his wife in the pool house, facilitate a sale, and figure it out. We can't predict every act of God or even scarier, acts of man, all we can do is figure it out as we keep one eye on the shot clock, the other on the goal – close the best deal for all and close it quick.

Now, at Altman Brothers we have developed systems for every part of a real estate close; listing appointments, feeding technology, broker's opens, price reduction, you name it. I break every deal into three basic phases:

1. Open
2. Work
3. Close

Even before they begin, phases 1 and 2 are aimed at negotiating a close. We have scripts to help with difficult calls; schedules for selling and price reduction; and tips for building agreement among parties, melting dissent, financing, finessing and finding new business to open, to work, to win, to close. We run cold opens constantly and flip them hot, ensuring a steady flow of business all year long. We strengthen all relationships – and I do mean *all* – into repeat business, the Holy Grail of commerce. With the Altman Close, everyone wins.

We never leave a deal on the table. We rarely say no. It is our job to ensure every offer is better for our client; always working toward the best possible outcome. Day in and day out we move toward a close and a commission check.

We pump up our opens. We offer tools that will ramp up the level at which we work every property. We set up our open with no room to fail. We're like a pack of wolves, and each member plays a role to keep me, the Alpha, alive and well, ready to feed first and make sure the rest are secure, the way I've planned all along. With the following pages, this will become you.

Take technology, for instance. I now breathe it. Almost 100% of all properties that change hands are seen on the internet first, and with that I come out swinging, positioning the house in its proper market before the first bell rings.

After years of success, "game time" and the "shot clock" are second nature to me. The Altman Close is in the air. I use these elements, and others you will read about in upcoming chapters – to my benefit. That's why I close almost every deal. I make money.

We are "Hollywood" ready, prepared to do what needs to be done – think, sell, facilitate, communicate, and broker a transaction equal (quite possibly) to an individual's entire wealth. Lives depend on me. My work matters. Do you want this as a real estate agent? Do you want to make money? If in your soul you need what we at Altman Brothers possess, the vicious hunger, then let's get moving. The clock is ticking.

But first, you must understand, despite a bit of drama and an occasional bite of my knuckles, *Million Dollar Listing: Los Angeles* often makes what I do look easy as I end each episode with my wide-eyed grin, a high-five with my brother, and a hug with my wife. The "easy" part is where the show gets it wrong. Closing is not always happy hour.

Closing, in truth, is often a bitch. Deals are difficult. Deals take work, lots of it. Deals take me from my family during dinner. They wake me at night. They interrupt me in the bottom of the 9th, the 4th quarter, my daughter's bath time. Deals require pleasing the most demanding creatures on earth – people. If it were easy, the clients wouldn't need us. They'd do it themselves. But not everyone's cut from that cloth.

Negotiating can be extremely uncomfortable for most people. Fortunately, as you know, I'm an animal who will barter in the trenches for my client, my coach, my business. Their money is my money and I will negotiate to the death to get us both the best deal possible before the buzzer sounds. I make moves or I lose. But I don't lose. I make money. I close.

To get what I want, to get what my client wants, and to even work with the opponent, there are triggers I use, a give-to-get, a give-and-take of what matters to me and what doesn't. Sometimes it's personal. Sometimes it's for the client. Sometimes it's just to get the deal done and keep moving. But it's always for the money and occasionally a bit of fun. I usually call those moments "Bad-ass, gangster shit. Ninja moves."

Last year, for instance, I was doing this deal on a teardown behind the Beverly Hills Hotel when I opened the garage to discover a 1974 Ferrari Dino. Immediately, I wanted that car. So, I worked it into my commission. In plain, it was awesome.

In another deal, I was flipping a house for a client who asked me if I could make a deal on some wristwatches for him. I didn't head to Canal Street in Manhattan for knockoffs, but I negotiated to acquire $9 million dollars worth of watches for $3 million. As long as it's legal, the Altman Brothers don't say no. Our mind is on pleasing, thus on closing, whatever the product may be.

If a property needs to shine, I have my team adjust the lights to look like Times Square. If we need to stage the home with furniture, here comes the Restoration Hardware truck packed and ready. Whatever may come our way, we don't say no.

If we were to leave offers on the table, we would lose money, so we leave nothing. We accept. We buy. We sell. We close. Everyone shakes hands. This is business and though often a hardship, it doesn't have to be a headache all the time.

We see agents drop out of the game all the time and we study their rise and fall. Why'd it happen? Where'd they go wrong? Constant variables take agents down, but a common theme stays the same: They mismanaged their set-up, their clock, or their team. They blew the play. Their open was garbage, their follow-through even worse, and as a result, the rest of the deal followed suit.

In order to have a successful play it takes follow-through from everyone on the team involved. Every aspect of every project needs to be timed accordingly. You can't miss a beat. After you open, you have to launch the property. Sales, marketing, social, digital, PR, tech, it all needs to hit exactly at the right time in the right order. Do it right, you make money. Otherwise, you're dead in the water.

You have to draw up the perfect play, rehearse it, execute it, and if need be, adjust, adapt, overcome. That's a launch, that's a close, and you only get good at it through trial and error, all pistons firing, everyone on the same page pulling their trigger when needed before the rest of the market gets a chance to catch their breath. If they see your blitz coming, the blockers come out. You hit the wall. Know how to adjust, adapt, and overcome.

We've built the Altman Brothers Company on our closes, and there's only one method that works toward the close: Put one foot in front of the other, busting your ass from A to B to C. No dancing around. We go straight at our goals, play by play, always with victory in mind. Our reputation is gold.

We feed our business with our success, investing in talent, education, technology, and innovation. We expand, explore, and conquer. We even launch new listings with drone videos now. Because of the internet, our reach is worldwide. We're localized globalists working with clients from Dubai, China, Russia, and the rest of the world.

This company is built on the deal – the open, the work, the close. We innovate. We reposition. We make deals. We make money. Our eye is on the clock, the playbook, and the field. We kick ass and we take names. We execute. It's the only way I know how to be, a master of time and information, data and desire, dreams, risk, fear and need. What can I say? I'm a closer and you can be too. You can make money. Let's play.

Chapter 3

MY FIRST CLOSE

I come from a family of closers, people who make money: Mom, Dad, older brother – closers. I used to joke I never understood how Dad ever landed Mom, but I knew all along it was simple. They were both quality people. He offered to share a great life with her as she too offered him. They shared the same values, the same dreams of family. They closed each other. I always admired that and wanted to replicate it someday. I have. But that's not the story here.

As for Matt, he'd kick my ass all the time as any older brother would, yet do it with love, and our competitive edge stayed supportive of one another. Also, being the younger brother I developed a better sense of humor than that stiff did. LOL. He's going to hit me for that.

Matt was always a role model to me. My parents instilled in him a work ethic that only made sense to admire. In school, I never quite caught his same flow, but I'd watch him on the field – soccer and football. I'd see his dedication, his spirit, his fight, his success. When Matt got into the University of Colorado to play football, I wanted something similar. I wanted the praise, the power, the pride.

But my mouth stood in my way. As you'll read later, one of my flaws was clowning. I had yet to learn the art of listening. In plain, I couldn't shut the hell up or stop busting balls or focus. This affected my football practice, which reflected in my performance. When I felt my football career was threatened, I knew I had to buckle down. I put my energy into the sport, but I still needed to gain that physical edge.

Seeing that football could lead me to college in the very same position as Matt, my mind was made up. But to do so, I needed work. I needed to improve. I needed to go to a football field-goal kicking camp to go beyond what Matt and my coach had taught me.

Being a smooth talker, while not always being smooth, came naturally to me, as it does for many Boston folks. Unfortunately, not as much as being a wise-ass. I'd play my parents one against the other for a new pair of cleats, or work on kids at the lunch table for baseball cards and comic books, their extra pack of cookies, what have you, but when I tried to sell my dad on my going to football camp during a time when the rest of the family was on summer vacation, he suddenly wasn't up to par with the dream I often supported. That's when I found myself in my first true nego-tiation, the first one that really mattered to me anyway.

Dad's no sucker. He'd recently busted me for sneaking a few beers with some friends; he knew he had me by the balls and he wasn't now about to go to bat for me against mom on this one. Especially since, if they were to still go on the trip, I would have to stay home alone, un-parented. After the Sam Adams lager incident, this seemed an impossible negotiation. Still, I gave it a go.

"Sorry, Josh," he said after I had failed another pop quiz, "Can't help you. Own your actions." I remember that word, "action." So action was what I took, pleading my case, desperate.

"Dad, you gotta let me go to football camp. How am I gonna get good enough to go Division I, like Matt? I need to be ready for senior year. Please, you can't do me dirty me like that. You can't cost me my life."

"You cost yourself." I had, but I wasn't done. I begged, telling him how bright my future would be, how he was ruining a career of glory. The man didn't care. He had heard this cry countless times from me in all forms. Matt too. As a great father, he knew how to stand his ground. I could see it wasn't my future he had in mind or so I thought. So, I made the argument about finances.

"Dad, please. Think about it. If I don't go on the trip, you'll save money."

"Nice one, Josh, but your mother and I are doing alright in the money department for now. Besides, you've proven you can't be trusted to be left home alone."

"Matt will stay with me. He doesn't care about the trip." Dad shook his head.

"It's called a family trip for a reason, son."

I huffed and I puffed, all out of arguments. That's when it hit me. I had violated the fundamental rule of all sales: Make sure the potential buyer knows what's in it for them. My football career did not include him, and the "save money" angle wasn't a current concern worth more than having us all together on vacation.

I had listened to him, how he said that he and mom "were alright in the money department." It set me thinking about another "department" of marriage. You see, my father was a workaholic gynecologist and a sex expert specializing in midlife sexuality, plus an author on both matters. You can check out his book *Making Love the Way We Used To or Better* (by Dr. Alan Altman), if you'd like. Mom was an extremely busy business owner, and I knew they barely passed by each other all week long, constantly falling asleep without one or the other home. It was a bold move, but I was older now, and we were talking man-to-man. I knew at once what was needed, the words blurting from my gut.

"If Matt and I don't go on the trip, then it's a couples getaway," I said. "A weekend of romance. Wouldn't it be nice to get away from the kids for a while, have a little time one-on-one? We're both men here, Dad. In your line of work, you know I'm right." I winked at him. He was taken aback, paused a moment, couldn't help but smile. He started to speak, halted, turned just a bit red and stared me down.

I had hit his sweet spot. The thing he wanted more than anything was some personal time with his wife, away from the office, away from the kids. I could give it to him. He could give it to himself. Easily. Happily. He took a breath, absorbed the thought. He looked past me, exhaled a sigh. "Goodnight, Josh." Dad kissed me on the forehead, still with a smirk on his face, and he went upstairs, but the seed was planted.

The next morning at breakfast before work and school, my parents conceded. Mom did the talking, a series of threats on trust and my social freedom. Matt would stay home and watch me. I shot Dad a grin, but he just played it cool, took another bite of his eggs. He must have pitched the idea to Mom as his own. The day was epic for me.

Closing Dad was my first big negotiation win, everything hung on selling him into agreement enough to talk to mom. The "what's in it for me" rule was burned into my brain from that moment on. If you want to close, make sure your clients know what's in it for them. That huge lesson helped me become "Hollywood."

By the way, Mom and Dad had a great trip, Matt wasn't stuck on a boring vacation, and I added 6 yards onto my kicking game, breaking a 50-yarder. Syracuse was in play. Everyone won.

Chapter 4

ALL IN WITH LA REAL ESTATE AND BRAVO TV

Right after college, Matt moved to Los Angeles. He felt the lure as many do. His first jobs were in the mailrooms of talent agencies. Soon he rose to become an agent with one of the world's top talent agencies: Creative Artists Agency, or CAA. He was making deals for famous actors, actresses, directors, and screenwriters, and he had just graduated from college. Mom and Dad were proud. I had to beat him … or at least join him. When I graduated and joined him out West, he got me a job … in a music management mailroom.

Now, in Los Angeles, Matt and I were again a team. We scraped $5,000 each together invested in a condo in West LA. It wasn't a great neighborhood then; we bought in before the influx of young movie stars who lamented about not being in walking distance of the bars, like they were back in New York. Months later, we flipped our first condo and I felt my first taste of the real estate market in the form of a paycheck. We had turned an actual profit.

From that point on, real estate had me for the rest of my life. I went from making $6.50 an hour in the mailroom to a $200,000 profit. We loved houses and we loved people. It was a natural transition. My hustle began. Only, it was working in a mortgage brokerage, with other people's money. Instantly I was successful. The struggle wasn't the business aspect; it was the set-up and follow through. But my family plus football had given me that strength in spades. Within a few years, by age 27, I was on my way to my second million. I was killing it.

Then the market crashed. If you don't remember 2007, you were either too young or you had nothing to lose. I did, and I lost it all. Everything. I was in a dark place, a real nightmare for a year and a half.

It was during that nightmare that a new dream formed. I'd *sell* real estate. I studied like a maniac what my mortgage business had already taught a lot of. But how would I get that first client? Where was the gap? Where was my in? What was I willing to do that no one else would? How would I open? The word buzzed through me: "open."

NEGOTIATING IS ALL

Immediately I began to sit open houses for other agent's listings. I became an expert at picking up clients; I even showed properties I didn't have. Still, nothing was popping off, but I knew never to quit. Six months and not one deal. I was sitting an open house near where I live now when Mitch and Mike walked in. I noticed them at once. They wanted a for-ever house in LA. I convinced them to give me a crack at finding it. After a relentless search, they settled on a piece of land I helped them buy for $1.6 million. They built their dream and the value today is off the charts, around $25 million, satisfying the greatest drivers of any real estate deal, emotion and money.

That's when I truly became the Shark. I was all-in. I was like the Matt Damon character in the movie *Rounders* – three stacks of "high society" against the Russian mobster Teddy, and on my way to Vegas. My Vegas. Hollywood.

From that point on, everything I saw became a negotiation. A friend wants sushi; I want a burger. Make the deal – raw fish it is, but I pick the movie. Matt wanted to watch the game downtown, but I was feeling a sports bar in Santa Monica. Make the deal, downtown it is, but he buys the beer. I knew what I was prepared to offer even before the exchange.

If you're like me, it doesn't matter if you're closing a huge deal or negotiating with your spouse for lunch, the same skills are in play: careful listening, strategic thinking, research, planning, presentation, points and counterpoints, possible outcomes, desired outcomes, acceptance or rejection. My shark's skin was thick and it only hardened after Mitch and Mike. I learned compromise and I swam straight for it, always on the hunt, memorizing every phase of every property as I passed by on the streets, in my car, no one or nothing off limits, a closer.

Let's get this straight; real estate *is* the close. Everything I do day in and day out is pointed toward that end. If you don't close, nothing happened. You've just moved a lot of paper around, made a bunch of calls, sent out emails, wasted gas, posted online, and walked a bunch of people through a house with nothing to show for it. Sure, you may have made some leads for the future, but you never want to be the agent that didn't close. You lose money. It sucks, plain and simple.

We're in a town that is one giant table covered in cash. I'm not about to leave it there for someone else to take. My brother Matt understood this even before I did. It was only a natural play for us to open up our real estate company, The Altman Brothers. We hit the ground running. Luxury real estate. No one could touch us and everyone noticed. Even BRAVO.

GOING HOLLYWOOD, TV TIME

Matt and I were killing it. I was killing it. But in a city of transplants from all over the nation, with all due respect to the locals, it seemed like everyone around me was on chill-mode. When you're an East Coast hustler with a fast mouth on a mission, running circles around these beach boys only made us stand out even more. If slinging multimillion-dollar properties was like waiting tables in a restaurant, the staff would have yelled at me to stop making them look bad. The management would have offered a promotion.

No one knew how to handle me when I'd walk into an open house, my fin above the water. Their muscles tensed, veins ran cold as they held on for dear life to their listings. All clients wanted a piece. The smart agents would flock to join me in sharing the feast. That's when the phone rang.

BRAVO heard about us and called, asking me to come in and audition for *Million Dollar Listing: Los Angeles*. This was to be the most important non-real estate close of my real estate career, kind of like me getting my dad to agree to football camp. This was national television. This was BRAVO. Matt and I knew what this meant for the business; this was the close of a lifetime. I was pumped.

As entrepreneurs we were well aware this could be a huge ongoing infomercial for our business. We went about building the close. Every move I made would be pointed at that BRAVO producer's final call, offering me the gig.

Because of our work at the talent agency, we had learned how television producers and executives think about TV. Matt and I dove into deep research, bingeing and analyzing every aspect of the show. We watched every second of the first three seasons, talking about character types and dissecting how they played off each other. The leads were a trust fund baby named Josh Flagg and the laid-back Malibu beach guy Madison. What this show needed was obvious to us; part East Coast street swagger, part business baller. I piss both elements, daily.

When I walked into the waiting room for that audition, there were what seemed in my head a hundred real estate agents sitting there. I waited and I waited and I waited. I never let nerves set in. Instead, I started channeling all my heroes – the biggest closers of all time who had changed the world for the better.

I know we're talking about a TV show here, but it mattered that much to me, and why couldn't this stepping-stone help me lead to changing the world – one property at a time? If you want to be the best you have to think like the best, believe you're the best, know you're the best. In that moment, I knew what I know every morning, what Babe Ruth knew stepping to the plate, Muhammad Ali in the ring, what Michael Jordan knew, the ball was going in. Seconds before walking into that audition room, in the forefront of my mind was Cosimo di Giovanni de' Medici. I'm serious and you should be too.

Let's look back at a pivotal moment in the history of modern banking: In the early 1400s, Cosimo de' Medici (son of Giovanni) convinced the leaders of Florence to adopt the financial system of maritime Italy, a monetary standard gaining momentum for commerce. The House of Medici soon became bankers to the world, or at least to the outer bounds of that empire, and patrons of the arts.

With an instinctive eye for beauty, Cosimo and the Medicis commissioned public art and architecture, some of the greatest of the Renaissance. Four hundred years later, millions still travel to see it. Florence and modern banking were built on Cosimo's close. In that moment, I was the big man himself, "The Elder" (Il Vecchio) as he was called, and these TV producers were about to know it.

When I finally heard my name, I took a double shot of espresso and felt the caffeine rush through my heart. A voice inside me screamed out as if from a spirit guide – the historic Notre Dame football coach Knute Rockne, the GOAT of coaching – "Blow this and you lose money. Kill 'em! Score! Win! Close!" It was Game Time.

I strutted into that office like it was mine, as if they were auditioning for me. I was on. "I'm Josh Altman," I said, "and I rule the Platinum Triangle." Eyes perked, jaws dropped. "I don't sell real estate, I wage war. My job is to get the best possible deal for my clients and I do it every time, for every one of them." I could see them lean back in their seats, already impressed with my confidence.

Unlike when I'm dealing with a buyer/seller, I gave them no room to talk: "One guy you have on the show," I said, "the guy up in Malibu, you call that negotiating? While he talks green smoothies, I've sold two multimillion-dollar houses and I'm showing a third. I eat guys like him before lunch."

Words just kept flowing. I actually insulted a few of their previous casting choices, another usual no-no in real estate. I was on autopilot until I ran out of breath. They knew I was done when I stopped spitting game. They thanked me, and I rolled right out of there on my Medici gondola like I had another important meeting to run to.

I called Matt. I told him I nailed it. Though to this day it wasn't me speaking. It was the spirit of Knute Rockne. I was the GOAT coach. I was Gordon Gecko in *Wall Street*. I was Cosimo de' Medici.

A week or so later, I was asked back. This time there were a lot less real estate agents sitting there. I kept with the strategy, this time with Steve Jobs and Los Angeles native Mike Markkula in the forefront of my mind.

For those of you who don't know, Markkula was the angel investor Steve Jobs got to put up the funds to build his first machines. Jobs found the guy – not always the easiest task and a huge part of the closer's job – who understood the idea of technology connecting the world, all the time, no matter where we were. It was Markkula's money, his management, and his marketing vision that laid the groundwork for Apple.

Again, my name was called. Again, I threw back two shots of espresso. My vision was nothing but end-zone as I stepped in front of the producers and launched my pitch, selling myself hard, stats and all, to make sure they knew I was the man for the job, to make sure they knew how I would benefit the show.

"I am the guy to bring edge to this show. I am the guy with the focus, the business experience and the sheer guts to bring this show to the next level. I am the guy to bring balance, balls, and no bullshit to *Million Dollar Listing: LA.*".

That's right. My closing strategy, the way I pointed the entire effort, was to explain, aggressively, how I could help them realize their dreams, a more successful show than it already was. In my work as a real estate agent, though always confident, I tend to be less cocky and egocentric, as you see on TV. Each close is different and requires an agent to adjust, adapt, and overcome. But for this my angle was straight on point – all Shark.

A few days later, they called me back. Then they called again. And again. Each time I stepped up with the auras around me – Einstein, Henry Ford, Thomas Edison, and the ever-present Knute "The GOAT" – I was building to close.

The process dragged out over a few months. I kept selling real estate and living my life until we neared an end, the final negotiation. I went back in and only a few agents were left. I was going to do everything in my power to make sure it would be me. I was all baller talk and real estate passion. Ultimately, they offered me the gig.

The call came shortly after the final audition. All the research, all the hero channeling, all the bravado had paid off. To say Matt and I were stoked was an understatement. We were out of our minds, floating.

This wasn't about being on TV. That was never my dream. This was about a strategic business maneuver for the Altman Brothers. We'd put into place an extraordinary piece of marketing that would propel us to even greater success. We didn't realize at the time how much greater that success would become. We just knew we were on our way.

All of this happened because I knew how to close in real estate. I knew my product. I knew my market, and I knew the kind of clients I was selling to. Even though I walked into that room and talked about myself, I was really talking about the show's needs. I was closing.

I had what it took to make that show rock. I took what's inherent to my personality – the love of engagement, service, risk, competition, and hustle – and blew it up big. I watched my counterparts' body language, facial expressions, and eyes. As they reacted, I adjusted. They were easy Southern California, so I was hard East Coast. I didn't have a trust fund; I had street smarts. I don't do smoothies; I do caffeine. I had already lost and remade a fortune on my own terms. I showed them what they needed for a successful TV show continuing long into the future.

Start reading from the beginning if you haven't realized this yet: I'm not playing a real estate agent on television; I'm a real estate agent being trailed by cameras. Cameras are there because I'm a closer. As I've said, I closed 189 deals last year; 10 were on the show. I'm not looking to win the lottery, I want to out-earn it. I want to open, work, and close.

I joined the cast of *Million Dollar Listing: Los Angeles* in the show's fourth year. Season 11 just aired. The mix of energies I saw when I watched those episodes all those years ago worked. The audience grew and grew. Week in and week out, my cutthroat, aggressive style, beat other agents to the bank over and over. And week in and week out, the audience shows up to watch the hustle.

Million Dollar Listing: Los Angeles was a life-altering close for the Altman Brothers. I will forever be grateful to the producers of the show and the BRAVO network. This business is full of closers. These guys – de Medici and Jobs – are obvious examples. They were just guys with big ideas. Their ability to convince that first person, the second, then the next and the next, was an essential skill. Nothing would have happened without it.

These closers left massive legacies that changed the world. I'm going to be like them. I'm going to be remembered. I'm going to change the world. You don't believe me? It's already happening. Take a drive around Los Angeles. See any construction? I did that. I made that happen. Einstein, Ford, Edison, Rockne, the greatest of all time? I'm going to be like them. Who are you going to be?

Chapter 5

RULES OF THE GAME: FIRST IMPRESSIONS

In real estate, for now, you may be playing on a smaller field than a medieval empire or the modern world, but make no mistake, you are transforming someone's life by helping them to move on from a house or find a new home to love.

Our homes are our castles, our sanctuaries, our worth, and our families. Our homes are often the greatest part of our wealth and have a huge impact on our day-to-day lives. Land, houses, vision, and investments are integral to the American dream. We all know it. We're all chasing our own dreams. Real estate is important work. Be part of it and it can fulfill your dreams.

No matter the money, the close is always the same. A $150,000 close is the same as a $50 million close. It just might have fewer moving parts to negotiate. Make no mistake. For some a $150,000 may be as critical, perhaps the sum total of one's wealth, as the $50 million deal may be to someone else. It's all relative. Be aggressive. Be hungry, whatever the task. You want the biggest bite for your client. Then you get your meal.

My nickname, the Shark, isn't based on a random shout-out during happy hour. I've carefully built my reputation as a closer since day #1. How? I make money. I break records. The numbers talk for me. The Altman Brother did $423 million last year. Boom! No argument. No need to brag. You want to make money? Then you want me. My stats set the tone for this book.

I represent athletes, entertainers, industry executives, start-up millionaires, and billionaires. They expect the best. A glance at my stats tells potential clients I handle high-priced, high-end, luxury real estate. The record-shattering prices tell them I close, and I close big. I waste no time, especially theirs. I deliver. I'm a beast.

Now, every real estate agent has at one time told a client he or she will deliver. It's part of the game. But in all my years of selling real estate, I've seen just three reasons why a deal fails to close:

1. Ego (buyer, seller, or agent)
2. Stupidity (agents getting in the way of/mismanaging the deal)
3. Something wrong with the house

The first two do not instill confidence. Let me explain. Stupidity . . . well, if I have to explain it to you, go back to page 1. As for ego, ego destroys what confidence builds. Ego is divisive. Confidence unifies. When ego kicks in, one of two things can happen. Everyone has a pissing match, or people shut down. Neither is good for business. In short, ego is for clowns. Don't be a clown. Be a closer. And as your wins pile up, be proud of your success. Let your stats speak for themselves.

But before your stats can pile up, before you can even set foot on the field, you need to know the basic rules of the game. This begins with you.

IMPRESSIONS MATTER

First impressions matter, whether you like it or not. You think that's shallow? Fine, you won't make money. But it's true, we size each other up all day all the time. A first impression happens in less than a second and is the most powerful influencer on how people respond to you.

In real estate, the open starts with the impression you make, the first imprint on a person's memory. Come in strong with confidence and style, and it will set the tone for the whole deal. The client will like what you give and they'll want to get more of it. Appearance rules – especially in Los Angeles. We're a visual town, and whether people want to admit it or not, the world agrees.

In a recent study, researchers observed 1,000 people during three-minute speed-dating sessions. The findings, presented at the Society for Personal and Social Psychology, revealed that people form their opinions in a fraction of a second, and no matter what evidence is presented to undermine that opinion, appearance trumps fact.

That means what you look like, the "uniform" you wear, matters. If you're dressed like a basketball player, you're taken seriously as a basketball player. If you're dressed like a golfer, you're most likely viewed as a golfer (or a preppy, country-club suburbanite). That's it. Get over it. Get a suit. Get a haircut. Shave if needed. Accessorize to fit what it is you're selling, and to whom you're selling it.

I make money for the mega-rich, so I want to act like the mega-rich. I look mega-rich – my suits, my car, my watch – therefore I am. Money talks, money shows, and we're doing this to make money. If this doesn't make sense to you, find a new line of work.

In this specific speed-dating study, researchers compared reactions to potential partners in videos as well as in person. They found that "passivity creates negativity," a downside of passive social tools. Great impressions are made in person. We're back to the old school: shake hands, make eye contact, and smile! Stay quiet and you'll be viewed as stupid, insecure, or elitist. That's it.

All that said, please, please, please, remember: although first impressions matter, especially as a real estate agent, this should never justify your dismissal of clients based on their appearance or current position in life. This is the flip side of the old adage "don't judge a book by its cover." You may think I'm contradicting myself in these past few paragraphs, but hear me out.

Everyone I meet, everyone you meet, is a potential client. I don't care if the person is sleeping on the Venice Boardwalk, is bad at bussing your table, or popping pimples in line at Starbucks. Treat everyone the same, everyone with respect and dignity, and do it because they are human beings. Not because you're trying to get dollars out of them.

If this is a problem for you, find another job, lose money, or stop being an asshole. Work on it. You never know when the little guy washing your car in torn '90s raver pants will become big and you'll be trying to sell him a house in the exclusive Bird Streets neighborhood of the Hollywood Hills after he stars in his first Marvel movie.

Respect is more than good business, it's good living, and it's being a quality person. Good people, good agents, and good clients don't have time for people who disrespect others based on shallow judgment. Nor should you. Stop enabling jerkoffs. Your job is to make money and to dress the part. It's not theirs.

I study psychology and human behavior to understand what drives my clients. I suggest you do the same. I find behavioral science more helpful than all the business books ever written, besides this one of course. (Just laugh. It's the way I'm wired.) I keep my head clear to observe what the client, what people, are doing and saying. Pay attention. It's in the details. That's where all the answers lie when you need to do your best job. How people think, how they move, it's all huge.

After a lifetime of studying cognitive bias and prospect theory – the latter has to do with how people make decisions based on the potential value of losses and gains – the Nobel Prize winner Daniel Kahneman identified two systems of thinking in his book *Thinking, Fast and Slow*.

"System 1" is the fast and intuitive approach. It's about automatic reaction and emotion. "System 2" is a slower approach based on rational thought, on deconstructing and analyzing one aspect of an issue against another; it's comparative.

Some people decide to buy a house in System 1; most get to System 2 before making a final decision. But as Kahneman importantly points out, research has demonstrated that poor decisions we make can also be traced to errors in cognition (System 2) rather than to corruption from our emotional thinking (System 1). In other words, System 1 can sometimes be logical and useful, while System 2 can produce irrational results.

But make no mistake; your clients' impression of you is all System 1, reactive and almost instantaneous. So is their reaction to a house. Liking the house is all System 1, and System 2 justifies the decision to buy. Your job is to help them formulate the conscious and deliberate approach of System 2 – and that includes helping them to sort out the useful parts of their System 1 reaction and the poor results of System 2.

That's the job. So present yourself in a way conducive to trust building and respect. If you want the checks I'm cashing, anything else is unacceptable.

10 RULES TO MAKE A POSITIVE FIRST IMPRESSION

1. No Narcissism, Ever

Runaway ego kills interaction. If a person says, "I just bought a ranch in Montana," and you reply with "I have an island in the Caribbean," you're NOT having a conversation, you're talking shit. Start a pissing match and you'll kill potential business. You'll lose money. Let clients tell you who they are and and what they want. When you open your mouth, gear your words toward what the client says and not whatever is running through your head. Be present.

2. Listen

This is right up there with #1. Shut up and listen. Los Angeles is full of wannabes and fakes who ask people questions just so they can cut them off and talk about themselves. Don't do that. Ever. During the open, you're already looking for negotiation tactics. Listen like your life depends on it because your business does. People can tell when they're being ignored. It creates a bad impression.

What is the client saying about how they want to price their house? Does it make sense, or are they delusional? Don't roll your eyes. Just listen. What house do they want you to find? How are you going to do that? You can't get information to close the deal if you don't listen. We'll touch on this again later. It's that important.

3. Kill the Jargon

"I'll execute a Right Angle Close," thought no one ever. It's ridiculous. Terms are fine for classrooms, but if you want to make money, then no SAT words. Talk normal. That's it. Simplicity. Transparency. Clarity. Done.

Fancy words used unnecessarily make you sound like a fool. You lose money. Industry jargon turns people off, and at best it makes them feel insecure about what they do and do not know. Jargon confuses and excludes. You're trying to make the whole deal easier for your client, your coach, not confuse or belittle them. Be real. Be confident. Be consistent. Be relatable. Be human. Or lose money.

4. Catch Their Draft

Psychological studies have proven beyond a doubt that human beings like other human beings who are similar to them. Like a racecar driver, just pull in line and do what they do – ride their draft. If you're talking to someone who speaks softly, calm your voice and back the hell up. Don't overwhelm. Don't be a poser. Always be yourself at your core. Faking a certain style to be cool is awful – like talking to a rapper and layin' on the slang – and when overdone it's really obvious.

But it is okay to pull right in someone else's lane as long as you're still you. It's a balance. Riding the draft is the beginning of "mirroring," a tried and true sales psychology you move into as the deal goes deeper. But let's not get ahead of ourselves.

With a new client, stand back, watch, and learn from them. Conversation is a dance. Don't jump in the mosh-pit if they're into ballroom. Ask questions and draw your clients out. Inspire them by asking about their goals, their dream house, what they like and don't. Once you know these things, you can sell them the property that meets their vision.

5. Dress the Part

Let's discuss this again. My clients move at a level that most of us could never imagine. They often belong to the 1% of the world's 1%. It doesn't matter if a billionaire meets me in board shorts and worn Vans, I come in a $3,000 perfectly pressed suit. I look good because I am good at what I do – closing deals and making money. I dress in a style that screams "success" because that's what I want to convey to potential clients.

At all times, I have clean shirts and ties in the trunk of every car. You'd think I'm ready to skip town. That's not it. I'm ready to open to close and in LA closing means looking sharp, not shaking hands with pizza sauce on my chest. I want the client to feel confident about my level of expertise, my success, and my effectiveness. I also live in the neighborhood where I do the most business. My watch is blinged out. My car, pimpin' – I fit in.

6. Act the Part

This coincides with #5. Some call this "fake it 'til you make it." But it's not the same as faking it or being a poser. In my last book, I discussed wanting to get in better physical shape. So you put on workout clothes, eat healthier, put your ass in the gym, and surround yourself with other people who enjoy exercise. It's about retraining the mind. That's it. You become what you want to be by being it, even if you're not top level yet. You'll get there, if being there is what you really want.

7. Compliment a Bit

As part of my open, I often compliment potential clients or listings, just a little, not too much. Don't freak them out. Look for the elements of the property you like and tell the owner. "I love the stone work." "That facade has incredible detail." "Wow, is that wooden mantle hand-carved?" We all love to have our houses appreciated. When you're meeting with potential buyers, listen to their needs and reinforce their opinions. Say, "You're smart to search in that neighborhood" or "with an important job like yours, you need to be close to the office." Such compliments are not creepy; they are pointed toward your shared objective – to make money! To close!

8. Make Eye Contact

This is basic standard advice for human interaction. It's Body Language 101: Look 'em in the eyes. If your eyes dart about as you talk, others will think you have something to hide or are checking the room for someone better to talk to. A second of eye contact is all you need. Meet the client's eyes before fixing your gaze on whatever it is they are talking about. Every few moments, again look them in the eyes. That's it.

If this makes you uncomfortable, or if you're fidgety, or if this is hard for you, get over it. Figure it out. Practice. Try finding a detail in the room and then move your eyes from speaker to object and back again in a slow, deliberate fashion. Whatever. Just give the client the respect of your attention. Look 'em in the eyes.

9. Rock Through It

No negative attitudes. If you're angry, don't show it. Smile. Feeling sick, fight through it. Smile. Frustrated with the client, remember your job is to close. Smile.

There was this incredible wide receiver for the Pittsburgh Steelers named Heinz Ward. No matter what happened in the play – dropped pass, a rough tackle, pass overthrown – the man smiled. Everyone liked him. All these other athletes are moping up and down the field, kicking over Gatorade coolers, and there's Heinz Ward looking like the Cheshire Cat.

Keep your attitude positive. No one likes a grouch. Energy attracts energy. Make it the good kind or you won't close. Shit, you won't open for that matter. You'll lose money.

10. Know Your Role

Do your job and be there to help, not to judge. Don't speak out of turn. Don't shame. Don't run your mouth. You are there to provide a service. You are the star, but remember, your client is the coach. People can be weird. Let them be. Love it. Enjoy it. Open and close.

During your first meeting with potential business clients, look for deeper points of connection. You're not selling, you're hanging out, getting to know someone, and humbly conveying your expertise. If I'm being shown a listing by a potential seller, I'm looking at the house, sure, but I'm also starting a relationship. The goal is to become their agent and work with them whenever they have real estate concerns for as many years as possible.

No one likes to be sold or hustled. They like being respected, understood, and worked with. Identify with your clients. Learn about them and let them learn about you. Get a beer together. Talk sports, kids, cars, pets. The business will come naturally; it's the reason you're both there to begin with. Turn a customer into a friend. Friends do business with friends who know their business well.

If you always act like a salesman, you will lose money. Grow your reputation through performance, customer relations, and follow-through. Have knowledge and passion for the community you work within. Be transparent, not shady. Friendly communication, respect, and hard work sells. Show up and show up on time, prepared. Look sharp. Know your players. Know your field. Know the shot clock. Let your stats speak for themselves. Do your job. Open and close. Build this reputation and more clients will come.

Chapter 6

THE DREAM TEAM: YOU CAN'T DO IT ALONE

You and you alone are now ready as an individual. Is that good enough? No. To get big, and I mean "Hollywood" Altman, private-jet-money big, you need a team. A solid team. A kick-ass team. A reliable, trusted, hungry group of wolves as poised, passionate, punctual, professional, and prepped to please as you are. You need your army.

Sure, you can start racking up the stats of closes by yourself, but if you want to really impress and blow the ceiling off this career of yours, then you need your people in place, ready to react. You will come upon that instant where you need to tell your client, "No problem, one second, I'm on it," at which point you break out the cell phone, call your guy, and know for certain you're going to get fire spit right back at you that equips you with the tools necessary to impress the hell out of every buyer, seller, and developer you deal with. I have my people, and they are invaluable to my process. I call my crew "The Josh Altman Dream Team."

I chose that name because of the "other" Dream Team. Remember back in 1992, when the international committee that sets the rules and standards of the Olympic Games first allowed the basketball event to include professionally paid players?

Prior to that time, only amateur players at the college level were allowed to participate, meaning the United States ranked average in performance despite being home to the best. Once this new rule came into effect, the United States was able to call upon the NBA in assembling what they called their "Dream Team," the best of the best – Michael Jordan, Larry Bird, Magic Johnson, Patrick Ewing, David Robinson, John Stockton, Charles Barkley, Kevin Malone, Chris Mullin, and Scottie Pippen – the 10 greatest basketball players of the time.

What do you think happened? The Dream Team killed it. They dominated. No one else in the world stood a chance. It was gold medals all around. This is what I have. This is what you need to be the best agent you can be. You need a "Dream Team" of closers, 24/7.

Surround yourself with partners, agents, support staff, mortgage brokers, bankers, title reps, contractors, and developers at the top of their game. You make them look good and they make you look like the best of the best, because you are. These pinnacle men and women you surround yourself with will help you close, close fast, and close efficiently. They will make you money. They know their business. They know the shot clock. They know when you call Game Time that it's time to shock and wow; time to impress and close.

One time I met a food mogul at a cigar lounge and sold his house by the next afternoon. His house wasn't even on the market. By the next day, I flipped his property for $9.1 million. Do you think I did it alone? Do you think I sprinted out of the cigar lounge to the office and started researching by myself? Hell, no.

Sure, I had some interested buyers in mind who were looking and I knew the style of properties they were looking for, but once the guy hinted he'd be interested in selling if I brought him the right offer, I was immediately on the phone with my Dream Team. The ball was already rolling as I showered away the smoke smell. The leads were in my inbox as I dried off.

I get business because the availability and accessibility I offer my clients is second to none. I answer and I text. Other agents don't. But an immediate response to a client would be nothing without the necessary information from my team. The Dream Team arms me with what I need, and as a result we all make money. I make them money. They make me money. We kill it.

My mortgage broker is the perfect example. Say I'm showing a $15 million house in the Hills on a Sunday evening and the buyer is returning to Korea that night. He wants to make an offer on the house then and there, and I know I need to strike while the iron is hot. Right then, I call the mortgage broker to work the numbers out. If that guy doesn't pick up my call on Sunday at 9:30 p.m., what happens? Nothing. We lose money.

Say I need my title company rep – and mine is a complete rock star –in the heat of putting together a deal. I can call my guy and say, "I need what's available in 90210, 800–900 block, for over $8 million with less than 500,000 outstanding" and BOOM! It's all in my inbox. Now I have the data I need to find the house to close the deal. It's priceless.

Finding these players isn't always easy. So what should you look for in assembling your team, besides the stats? Surround yourself with positive Type-A colleagues whose energy is a good compliment to yours.

"Ambitious" and "Type-A" are compliments in my world. Do they share your passion for people and real estate? Are they confident about themselves and their work? Can they perform under deadlines and other pressures? Do your clients like them? Are they reliable? Relentless? Are they problem-solvers?

Listen, this career is war. It's battle. Who do you want on your side when the shit goes down? These people are your platoon in the trenches. If they don't have your back at a moment's notice, any time of any day, if they're not prepared to take aim and shoot, then you lose money. Another agent will pick up your paycheck.

There's a saying, "success breeds success," and it was recently put to a reality test. The National Science Foundation underwrote a study analyzing online data as it related to career. They found that people who achieve more receive more opportunities, and in turn create more success.

For the Altman Brothers, our first wins were on the football field. Then Matt became a talent agent at CAA, the biggest talent agency of the time, and I built the mortgage business. We used those first successes to reach buyers and sellers when we started our agency. We used that same method in building our Dream Team. Many are still our clients and our team has only grown stronger. Every day we build on what we did yesterday, reaching to beat our personal bests, doing bigger deals with more speed, efficiency and skill. We're killing it.

Now, not everyone can hold all the details of a deal in their head like I can, I just have a memory for numbers. Being the "Rain Man of Real Estate" means you stay in close touch with your list of closes. My Dream Team does this for me and I do it for them. Not only does this build confidence for all, but it will also remind you what you do well and where you need some work. You'll see patterns of strengths to celebrate and misfires to correct, both in you and the team. Keep refining. Closing leads to closing just as success breeds success.

But learn how to please your team or you risk a coup. Don't piss off the people who keep you at the top of your game. Remember the second reason why deals often go wrong – the agent gets in the way. This can happen when you're team doesn't feel secure or appreciated. Not establishing trust in a business full of doubt will bite you in the ass.

Trust is critical in driving business, and since the recession of 2007–08, trust has been dropping among professionals across all industries throughout the world. You must establish trust and reinforce it constantly. All the dogs get a bone, all the time. The more they play, the more they get fed. As does a client, your team needs to know they are on the best team, that it is in their best interest to stay working with you. There are three easy ways to ensure this:

1. **Be consistent.** Do what you say you'll do. Follow through. We base what happens in the future on our experiences in the past. Don't be a flake. Lose trust, you lose your team. Lose your team, you lose money.

2. **Closing reputation.** How you convey your abilities (and those of your team) creates trust. My stats have been built because of the stats of my team. I advertise for them, they advertise for me. A client trusts me because of my stats and my brand. If I tell them, "Ah I got this new guy, let me see if he can . . ." Then they're shook, uncomfortable. They're not secure. If I say, "I'm calling my guy who is the best of the best, watch this . . ." and that person follows through, then everyone feels rewarded and respectfully acknowledged.

   The client knows without again asking, that my team is in place, this is who they are, and they're the best. This client will return. The same goes for the team. If I waste their time with consistently no-good clients, I lose my trust with them. They won't answer my calls when I need them to. If I lose the trust of my team, I lose money.

3. **Express solidarity.** People trust people who they feel are on their side and who have partners in place who are also on their side. My family – Matt, a closing beast, and my wife Heather, a half a billion dollars of sales on her own – have proven our business is more than just a team in the office, but a team in life.

   This brings comfort to clients as well as to our Dream Team, who are very much now considered part of the Altman family. Our business is family-owned and operated. We've got each other's backs. This makes clients and our Dream Team feel secure.

Trust comes from a lifetime of interaction. I understand that most people do not have such a strong foundation as my wife and brother to work with in building their Dream Team, but agents are only as good as their supporting players. Up your game by packing your immediate vicinity with closers, people who get it done through their abilities, positive personalities, and perseverance. Focus the work on closing on your clients needs by meeting your team's needs. Promote your success by promoting your team. Everyone gets their cut and will come back for more. There are coaches that win and there are coaches that treat their players well. Be both and you'll keep making money.

Chapter 7

FRESH EYES ON THE PRIZE

You're not the same agent you were when you first picked up this book. Your mentality, your sense of urgency, your approach, your look – it's now baller. You're a killer. An animal. Your heart beats for the deal. You are on your way to being "Hollywood" in the Altman sense of the word. So let's look at the basics, a refresher of the job format – open, work, close.

This is Los Angeles, the home of film and television, the land of scripts. The traditional storytelling and screenplay format – beginning, middle, and end – applies to the work of a real estate agent. You don't need to be Shakespeare, James Cameron, or even Josh Altman to get this one down. We're not reinventing the wheel. We're setting up to close in three acts.

For the agent, Act I is the open, the get-the-listing moment when you learn about the owners and the house's history or the house shopper's dreams. The open creates opportunity so that action can happen. You enter the scene. You analyze the set-up. You break it all down, considering every angle based on the client: who they are, how they are, what they

45

want, what you can do for them. If it's the property you engage first, you size that up in the same manner.

You need to prove that you're the agent for the job. You have to open, to present clients with a course of action. You have to give them what they want. This can be a pain. We humans are demanding creatures. We are skeptical, full of doubt. We constantly think someone is trying to get one over on us, yet we still want what we want. We need to be confident and secure that the superstar agent we have hired has our best interest in mind.

You have to convince and catapult the client into action, to assure them you will fulfill their goal. Opportunity has presented itself because you have presented opportunity.

Another of my favorite films – Scorcese directed this one too – is *The Wolf of Wall Street*. Leonardo DiCaprio stars as Jordan Belfort in this true story about a closer, a kid from New York who has no money but is desperate to make it. He quickly learns the ropes and acquires the salesman's golden touch, selling penny stocks. He sees a gap in the market and decides take action, to go for it, setting up his own firm based out of a garage and manipulating others into buying, buying, buying. He finds a partner. The end of Act I is this set-up into action. Belfort and his partner are off and running, hustling, selling.

Cut to Altman action: I meet a mega-rich client, a man who tells me he doesn't play games. He has little time. He wants a certain property in the Hills. I take aim and go for it. I launch into action, propelling us both into Act II, the meat of the story. The work. The hustle. The middle.

Act II holds the drama. Characters are pounded with challenges they must overcome. In this work phase, I'm constantly learning and adapting, just like a character in a movie. Here's where you encounter the personalities and ways to approach them.

Take in all the information around you: What are people saying about the house? What are the comps? What leverage can you use to achieve your goal? How does the neighborhood figure? What does the client's manner tell you? How does this affect what you do? How do you keep refining your work? There are endless negotiations and tiny deals working toward the big close. It's impossible to give this phase a precise name. So it's *work*, negotiation and closing little deals into one final one.

In *Wolf*, DiCaprio's character now has his eye on the prize, his goal – money and lots of it. He's bobbing and weaving to make it happen, cash coming in hand over fist. His business grows. At the midpoint, Belfort reaches a milestone of success – the stunning wife, the mansion, the cars, the yacht. He is winning, but the plot thickens; the game changes.

Here's a moment when the *Wolf* analogy departs from the Shark's game: Belfort was breaking the law to make his money: lying his way to success, ripping people off, selling them stocks that didn't quite exist. The Feds take notice. Now the goal is to stay out of jail but still make more money, a challenge he thrives on. He finds new angles, learns how to cover his tracks. He moves forward – new strategies, a new business model – into a new plan.

No matter how the game changes for the Altmans, we don't break the law. But when the plot thickens, we still need a strategy.

My client in the Hills has just chosen his property. I'm in the trenches, fighting for this house. I meet with the sellers. No problem, it's an easy sale – if he wants only half of the property. In my Act II, I learn that the property my client wants is actually two different lots being sold separately. At the price he desires, he can either have one or the other. This is not an option for him. He wants both.

Now, for Matt and me, the task is to massage this seller into parting with both lots at a reasonable price. Also, our client needs to come up in his price, rethink what he is willing to spend. The seller won't budge nor will our client.

What we thought we were dealing with no longer exists. Our back is against the wall. If we don't make a move we lose the deal, we lose our client, we lose money.

I research the people, the property, and the neighborhood. Hard. The more information I have, the more effective I'll be at the close. This is the phase were I develop strategy all pointed toward the best possible outcome for my client. Now we call other clients. We show this seller what most are willing to pay for each home, the reality of what he will get for one property versus what he could actually get for two and be done with it all, no more nut to carry. It's not good enough.

If you've opened well and understand your client and/or a specific property, you'll have a good sense of the direction of your work. Remember how I pointed the *Million Dollar Listing LA* audition? I studied hard and isolated exactly what I was selling: an agent to play off the other on-air agents, throwing heat to attract and build viewership, because that's what the producers needed.

With any listing you must ask yourself, how will I point this close? How will I conquer this? Do you already know other right buyers or houses for this client? Does it have to be this property? Can I direct this client elsewhere?

What if you need to generate more buzz – to get people talking? Do you leak information to real estate press? On social media? Or through influencers and word of mouth?

Because most of our clients are athletes, entertainers, industry execs and founders, buzz is not hard to generate, though these clients usually insist on extreme privacy. We respect this and uphold their request, usually by signing non-disclosure agreements (NDAs), but privacy for the famous is often unattainable. The right buzz, the words that get buyers into the house, is part of our refining our work as we go.

An example of this is my work with Kim Kardashian West. Everything she and her husband do generates headlines. From selfies to hip-hop, fashion to television, they are famous as hell. We sold them a house in 2013 and then sold it for $8 million more when they sold it to a Russian billionaire. That owner recently had a child and decided to go for a bigger house, so we're representing the sale again. We just sold it. It worked out, but in such a personally stylized house, how did we get the right buyers interested in a home that has been for sale twice in eight months?

We find new buttons to push and dangle mysterious transformations they have to see to believe. Let the clients be exclusive, the select few who tour the house in what is sure to be a brief time on the market.

So I picked up the phone and turned on the heat, pitching this house to every lover of modern architecture who could afford it. The "buzz" of this house was what Kim and Kanye West did with it; they oversaw every detail of its transformation. It's now a monument to minimalism with a huge repositioned outdoor swimming pool, floor to ceiling automatic windows, panoramic city views, white on white lines, and a new entrance into what Kim called "the glam room." Who wouldn't want to see that?

I threw down the gauntlet in an interview with a big website by saying, "It's one of those houses you're immediately gonna fall in love with, or don't get at all." I wanted every house buyer in Los Angeles who loved contemporary design to be intrigued by this house and want to see it. The right person will be inspired by it, as the Russian was, and want to call it home.

The more energy you get swirling around a house, the more action you'll see on the work side. The more action you create on the work side, the odds are you'll have a more competitive close, and competitive closes mean multiple offers, hopefully over list. That's the sweet spot of every real estate deal.

Work comes at you fast and fierce. It's important to analyze and formulate a strategy that you can revise as you go. If you represent the seller, your work should be pointed at gathering multiple offers to drive the price as high as the market will accept. If you represent the buyer, you want to negotiate the lowest price possible. Some clients have other motivations besides money; they don't want the house demolished or want a house in a neighborhood that has no inventory. Work is when you have to catch whatever ball is thrown at you.

Now we move into Act III, the resolution, the close, where we hope everyone lives happily ever after. My goal with my buyer in the Hills has changed. I've now generated enough buzz around the two homes he wants that I force his hand. The pressure is on, others want the property. Although the client may not be pleased that his dream home(s) are under threat, I have set myself up to win one way or another, but my goal is always to please my client.

To do this, I have to successfully show the seller that his dream of flipping both properties for his desired price is unreasonable. Besides, the other interested parties only want one of the houses, not both, as my original client has demanded. I need to pull the trigger. I need to finish this up. So too does Jordan Belfort.

In Act III of the film, Belfort is no longer able to continue his business. He needs to soften his financial losses. He needs to stay out of jail, but that's no longer possible. He has to face the hard truth. He needs to take what has happened and cut a new deal, turn it into something positive. For the Wolf that was a memoir and, after prison, a new career as a motivational speaker, sharing stories of success and failure.

So too do my client and the seller of the two properties need to face the truth in Act III. Months have dragged on. Carrying costs have added up. Time for once is on our side. It doesn't make sense for the seller to only sell one property if he can sell two, even at a loss.

I renegotiate once again, presenting the reality of the situation to both my client and the seller. If they want to salvage something from their dreams, then they will need to find a positive outcome. They need to close. The deal is done. The movie is over.

But is a trigger always necessary? No. In my experience, if someone is going to offer on a house, they offer on a house. What you do with that offer, how you manage it, is the difference between a backseat driving agent and an agent-driver. I get behind the wheel of every close and get everything I can out of it; my clients expect nothing less.

The term for this is "integrative bargaining," and it's the gold standard of negotiation as worked out and described by Harvard Law School professor Roger Fisher and his co-author William Ury in the 1991 book *Getting to Yes*. In my language, this type of negotiation can be summed up with "you've got to give to get." This isn't haggling over price; this is actual give and take on deal points such as all cash versus loans, type of loans, repairs, and so on.

Negotiation starts from the door, and this often means negotiating your commission time and time again. You think it's fixed, right? Try telling that to a multimillionaire client who is power-hungry. Not always easy. I usually give up what I don't care about to get what I do. It's simple negotiation. What matters more to my client and me. Negotiation is rarely simple and it starts with the open.

As one of my clients likes to say, "The harder you work, the luckier you get." I believe it's possible to create luck everywhere I go – whatever I do. I'm always looking at real estate, meeting new clients and refining my skills. I study data on neighborhoods and read real estate gossip as the sun rises. The three-act formula is straight up.

Open + Work = Close

I organize ideas and experience into two distinct parts, then move toward the climax, the sale. The moves inside the close are crazy, ever-changing. You never know who is going to throw what at you, and I draw on different skills and knowledge with every new client. Change is the only consistency.

You as an agent on the field need to be prepared to adjust, adapt, and overcome at a moment's notice, your Dream Team on standby, sharks swarming, ready to attack. Open. Work. Close.

Thump your chest to it. Open. Work. Close. Say it with each thud on your heart, just like you're Belfort's mentor, played in the movie by Matthew McConaughey. Open. Work. Close. Open. Work. Close. This is your mantra. This is your being – open, work, close. This is your body and blood. Open, work, close. Boom. Boom. Boom. Open, work, close!

Chapter 8

ALL ABOUT THE OPEN

Y̶ou can't close if you can't open. That's it. No client, no listing, no deal. You have to start the game. If you can't land a client or a listing, go home. Your mission, your only mission, is to sell a property to or for someone.

There are as many ways and places to open as there are people. As you become established in a market, opens come from all directions. I've opened deals in grocery stores, hot tubs, taco truck lines, the gym, pools, restaurants, charity events, concerts, the veterinarian's waiting room, baseball and football games, and even – sometimes – my office. Keep in mind that where there are humans, there is the opportunity for business.

The Altman Brothers have huge reach because we have to; our market demands it. People from all over the world work and invest in Los Angeles. I search for buyers and sellers at the top of the financial food chain – Asia, Europe, the Middle East. Celebrities fly in at all hours of the night, looking for exclusive showings before the sun rises. My product is hyper-local but my clients require me to think like a globalist. That means information about world markets. That means the internet. That means messages have to resonate in Southern California as well as the rest of the world; our listings are translated into 20 languages. We open everywhere. We close in LA.

So how do you find real-live clients to open? We're not there yet. Calm down and listen.

If you're in the beginning stages of your career, I suggest you do what I did: Sit at other agents' open houses. That's how I snagged 6 of my first 10 deals. Potential buyers who want those homes are fair game for anything you might offer them. Engage. Ask pointed questions about what they want and go find it for them. But you're still not there, not yet. Let's look at how much you really have to offer.

The ocean is a lot bigger than you think. To be truly prepared for your catch, you need to search under every rock. Not for the client, but to get a feel for the territory first.

KNOW MORE THAN THE 'HOOD

If you meet someone and they express interest in a particular neighborhood, you'll need to draw on what you know is available. You need to be sharp, quick, ready, always something more to show. You have to flood your client with options ready to spit at them. "Don't like this one? Check out that one! Not for you? How about this? Have you ever considered . . . ?"

You must be ready to sell real estate 24/7, know your market inside and out, and keep studying. "Your husband loves art deco, but you want Spanish tile? Here is three of each with something in between. Oh, you're pregnant? These five offer outdoor spaces with an extra bedroom in a great school zone, the neighborhood up and coming." Patrol the waters, have an ear to the street. A jackhammer sounds around the corner. You check it out. A coffee shop opens in the hood? Circle the block. You need to be a property stalker.

If you see a guy in a $3,000 suit jumping out of a bush in the Hollywood Hills, it's probably me. I'm a self-admitted property stalker and I make it a habit to learn about a new neighborhood, a few blocks, or even a specific property, every week.

Through my Dream Team title agent I can find all the information I need: Has the house has been on the market for three months with no sale? Odds are the listing agreement is about to change. I need to know that if I'm going to represent a buyer or a seller. It's a whole lot easier to negotiate a lower price if you know no one is beating down the door.

Properties that haven't been on the market for decades can make awesome deals. Unless it's a castle in Europe, most houses don't stay in the family. I keep my eye on these properties because when they hit, vultures circle and I drive up the price. If I get to it first with one of my strategic alliances, we can redo the property and make a profit.

I have a house in Beverly Hills right now that's been in escrow for a year, waiting out the lifetime of the elderly owners. I know, it sounds creepy, but it's not. It's business. It's reality. If you haven't heard, life will kill you. I'm just being aware and doing the math. I'm giving myself options. In a seller's market, if you see a listing on the market past 120 days, a change in real estate agents may be coming. More math, more options. Be aware and you'll bring your clients what they never saw for themselves. You'll make money.

That said, just like property owners, cities are constantly changing and you have to be ahead of them. You have to be aware all of the time. You have to predict. You have to see the trends. You have to open and close. You have to be a fortuneteller: There are signs everywhere to make you look more psychic than you actually are.

Real estate agents can lose sight of the transformative effect they have on their town or city. You're making and remaking neighborhoods by the simple fact of who is buying and selling. I am literally changing Los Angeles and the world one property at a time.

Bringing in higher income, educated buyers to marginal neighborhoods filled with "fixer uppers" is the very definition of gentrification, and it's driven by buyers, sellers, developers – and their real estate agents. Driven by me – and driven by you if you're good enough.

San Diego and Philadelphia currently lead the way with gentrification in America. That's how real estate agents change cities. *Governing* magazine said that in Philadelphia from 1980 to 2000, only 1.5% of the city's poorest neighborhoods were upgrading. By 2018, 28% were gentrifying. Do the math: That's a jump of 1,800% for Philly, and only San Diego registers higher. Communities rise from the ashes because of you and me.

At the end of the day, I used to drive home to the Bird Streets in the Hills. Construction equipment made the trip slow as hell. I'd bitch a lot. One day my wife Heather said, "You did all this. These trucks are here because of you. Stop bitching about traffic. You created it."

She's right. If we're doing our jobs correctly, the landscape is always changing. It was the first time I had a true sense of how the Altman Brothers shape Los Angeles. Because it was my hood, I knew all the moves already and forgot how much of it was my doing. The trick is to notice in the other communities where you're not already killing it. Pay attention. You need the vision ready to sell your client even before you have the chance to open them.

Speculation about "the next hot neighborhood" is endless in real estate and hugely useful to younger buyers looking for their first "starter" home. Real estate agents in search of new worlds to conquer or young agents who want to begin building a career are great neighborhood builders. If you have strong developer relationships, you'll hear about up-and-coming neighborhoods, the "under-stored" areas where they see "green shoots" of growth indicating something new is taking hold.

In Park Slope, Brooklyn, 20 years ago, that green shoot was Connecticut Muffin, a coffee shop with a suburban clientele. In their quest to identify new markets for hot drinks and baked goods, Connecticut Muffin found a home among some "nesters" in New York City, young growing families that had flocked to the area, driving prices into the multiple millions for a simple brownstone.

Today, celebrities such as Michelle Williams and Anne Hathaway have houses there, and Matt Damon just bought what may be the priciest piece of private real estate in Brooklyn's history, a penthouse just shy of $17 million. The real estate agents and developers who brought Park Slope into the twenty-first century are the best people to get you into that community; they know it, hell they built it, and they've heavily networked it.

After living and selling the Bird Streets in L.A., little goes on there that I don't know about. As the Bird Streets rose, I did too. It's the same in Park Slope. Understand what's hot and what's not. Use your expertise to gauge real estate on the rise and on the fall; that's part of your reputation building and market understanding.

Read local business news to anticipate ways that your town and neighboring communities will change. Watch major commercial players and see what they do. When Google moved into Venice Beach in Los Angeles, it was obvious what would happen. Jim Morrison once squatted tripping on acid where some of the priciest real estate in the land now exists.

If you get the signs right, if you can read the up-and-coming locations surrounding the community you are already serving, you will make money. Use this talent as part of your stats. Put it in your bio – fortuneteller!

When Matt and I started out, we were flipping houses in Silver Lake, Los Angeles. It was filthy and full of gangs, but we saw the signs. We saw the artists, the new cafés. Now it's high-priced, super trendy, and full of young movie stars. We were in Silver Lake because that's what we could afford. We rose with the neighborhood and were able to offer the area to others who couldn't see the upswing. It worked.

Imagine if a few years ago you had early insider information that the St. Louis Rams were moving to Inglewood, Los Angeles, a neighborhood once full of racial tensions. You'd be killing it right now. The new NFL stadium will be ready in 2020 and real estate prices are off the charts. Now, with the new stadium, here come the Olympics, the World Cup. Here comes money. If you own there, life looks good about now. If you're an agent selling it, congrats, but watch your back. The Altman Brothers are just up the 405.

WATCH YOUR BACK

There are a million ways to screw up an open. I see agents do it every day. In fact, I rely on agents who blow their opens. It's part of my strategy. I look for their flaws, their weaknesses, their misses, and I strike. From the clients' point of view, when I roll in with my stats and point out what their agent is doing wrong even before they've done anything, it's very hard for them not to want to lay down with me. I bank on it. It works.

Mess up? Lose the client. Someone like me will get them next.

Don't land them immediately and hold on tight? Lose the client and again, someone like me will get them next. It's that simple.

The Altman Brothers feel quite comfortable allowing our clients to stroll properties by their lonesome, but I don't suggest you allow this yourself. It's blood in the water, man, and I can taste it. The entire world is waiting to be opened and I'm ready to close 'em. You need to be, too.

A few words about "guarantees" in real estate, so don't say I didn't warn you.

There is no "given" when representing a buyer. A buyer's agreement has been obsolete for years in my market. Never forget that a buyer works on a moment-to-moment lease breakable at any time by either party. It's not unlike dating.

You have to win the person over, prove yourself every time before someone else comes sniffing, making false promises, looking for their in. Buyers are free to leave at anytime. So, you have to make sure they know there is no reason to be with anyone else in the room but you.

The only "official" open is the seller's agreement. With the seller, well that's marriage, baby. There are legal ramifications if you split. There's lots of drama with buyers and sellers alike, but there can be a lot of lovin' as well.

NETWORKING AND GIVING TO GET

Take the largest industry in your area – for us in Los Angeles, that's entertainment – and do your best to network it. If the biggest employer in your town is the hospital system, for instance, go see employee services and introduce yourself.

Look for places where people in transition hang – I'm talking the big events here: birth, marriage, divorce and death – and meet them. These pivotal life moments often require new living space. Talk to wedding planners and wedding dress boutiques, divorce attorneys, jewelers, obstetricians, probate and estate lawyers, and liquidators.

When Heather was pregnant with Alexis, Lamaze class was a great place to open. When Alexis was born we moved out of the Hollywood Hills. I was ripe for what a good real estate agent would describe as the "open" of life transitions.

As far as your own community, I can guarantee you that you're not working it enough. Dirty up to help clean and dig in. Google national and hyper-local social activism groups and business development organizations. Find out who is doing what charity and where. Join. Be part of what you sell – the community.

Matt and I have done a lot of volunteer work over the years and one of our all time favorites is pet adoption. I also got involved with the Wounded Warrior Project through a friend and client, Mark Wahlberg, and it brought a cool new dimension to my life. These projects are personally satisfying in the moment and professionally valuable for the future.

You want a good laugh? Watch the rap video *I Sell the Dream* on YouTube. I'm like the Drake of real estate, and all proceeds went to the organization.

Form your own group of "leaders" who get together regularly to discuss anything from neighborhood development to football. The point is to gather, network, let everyone know you sell real estate, and you have a property in mind for them when they're ready to discuss it.

These charity group "leaders" can also provide you with ever-important real estate gossip. As a city, town, or neighborhood changes and evolves, your group may know it before it hits the street because, in real estate, if you read it in the paper, it's too late. Information is gold. Information is power. Information is the open, the work, and the close.

Now that I have a baby girl, I can see how networking opportunities will arise at future events: peewee soccer, parents' night at school, ballet classes, play dates, and family barbecues. My life will be filled with people who have children and in real estate, children means growth.

Growth means upgrade; upgrade means a new house. You can be the guy who upgrades all. That's the main element of being "baller." offering people the possibility of improvement. We are "middlemen" in more ways than one. Need a bigger house in a better neighborhood? I can make that happen.

One Saturday afternoon, I had a listing appointment, a big one, for a potential client who wanted over $50 million for his estate. I left the meeting and was wandering the aisles of Ralph's grocery store in my pricey suit, looking ridiculous among shoppers wearing the yoga pants, and gathering items from my wife's list. I leaned into the cold case to grab the frozen chicken nuggets – you parents of toddlers know what I'm talking about – and I heard someone call my name.

An old client stood behind me, three tiny kids filling her shopping cart. When I found her first condo years prior, she was still single. Now, her husband was a rising star at one of the studios, and they were thinking about a home upgrade. Their number of children demanded it.

Within days, I had her completely in love with a five-bedroom in Manhattan Beach, one of the strong school districts in Los Angeles's South Bay. This place was on the edge of a park and had a huge backyard, especially for that part of town. The outdoor space was money – pool, firepit, and built-in seating. It was perfect for entertaining her husband's new industry colleagues and all for around $5.3 million.

I passed them the keys two weeks later, all because I bumped into an old client in the grocery store and asked, "Where you living these days?" I opened. I opened ready to close. I asked questions. I engaged. I began the deal.

I don't sit in my office to work: I go to the Beverly Hills Starbucks and hand my card to people I talk to in line. I say, "I'm Josh Altman. It was great talking to you, man, and if you or your friends ever have questions about real estate, hit me up." I offer to answer questions about real estate, not sell a house, because when I open, I give to get.

Giving to get makes money. The ancient Babylonians knew that when they wrote the Code of Hammurabi, and believe it or not, some 4,000 years later, there's a science to back this up.

Robert Cialdini, a professor emeritus of marketing and psychology at Arizona State University, explains the reasoning behind why people say "yes" his classic book *Influence: The Psychology of Persuasion*. If you haven't read it, do. It makes sense, and the theory makes money. Remember, we're here to make money, so listen up!

Cialdini isolated six points that work – whether consciously or unconsciously – to shape decisions. The first one is reciprocity. To prove this, Cialdini created a simple experiment in a restaurant to determine if the gift of a mint would increase tips.

Servers who left a mint with the check saw an uptick of 3% in what customers left them. When the servers said, "Here are two mints for you," the tip didn't double, it quadrupled. The next round of the experiment had the servers put down two mints, walk away from the table, stop, return and say, "For you nice people, here are three mints." Tips were off the charts, coming in at an average of 23% higher.

That's why you should always offer help, advice, kindness, and respect; it's an open, maybe a bit slower than a buyer on the line, but it's an open nevertheless. It's "giving to get," and "giving to get" makes money. Open. Work. Close. Make money. Got it? Get it? Good.

Chapter 9

OPEN HOUSES FOR CLIENTS, BROKERS, AND INSIDERS

Congrats. You opened a client. You landed a listing. Good for you. Don't you dare celebrate yet – I don't see a commission check.

You've just started out, and you've got no reason (and not enough clientele) to be exclusive with this property. You've yet to generate the buzz. So you create some. You host an open house.

Contrary to the belief that to kill it in real estate you have to master the proverbial real estate bible, to be a solid agent you have to become an expert on people – reading moods, body language, hesitations, and silences. So sharpen your powers of observation at these events, and learn from the experience. Let's start with your basic client.

DON'T TOUR, SELL

You've seen the clients leaning forward as they tour the house, nodding as they go. They smile and focus. They ask questions. They ponder, express interest, and sometimes straight up pretend to know what they're looking at when they haven't the slightest clue.

Some are authentic in this, some just want so badly to be pros, others not to look stupid. You can see it on their faces. One way or another they see themselves living there, happy. It doesn't matter what they're really thinking. What does matter is that they are there, ready to be worked, and it's your job to work 'em. These people are your target market. They're your bulls-eye. Open 'em, work 'em, and close 'em.

Every open house has curious seekers, or Sunday drivers who spot the sign and stop in. I've met more than one person who was like Jason Segal from the 2009 movie I Love You, Man, driving the hills in UGGs, looking for open house signs because their subtext says "free food here." A dude like that can generate buzz, and so can the neighbors. Fools or not, talk to them with the same enthusiasm you'd pitch a buyer or the press. Treat everyone with respect. Do the job. Sell the house as if you would love to live there.

As for the serious buyers, I've worked a lot of open houses where a random meeting turned into a close. It happens. Be ready. Be prepared. Opening to close is the goal. Touchdown. Done. Go have a drink. Then, do it again.

Your job there is to make an impression. Sell the home. Capture names. Close the deal. Make money! The term "open house" has the word "open" in it for a reason; use the opportunity. Sell. Open. Work. Close.

Your job is NOT to be that annoying cliché of an agent who sits in the kitchen, disengaged, and plays on the phone. Be that person and someone like me will take your client. You'll lose the sale. You'll lose money. Someone like me will make that money.

I worked with a young agent once and asked him to show me his listing. The kid takes me on a lame-ass museum tour, pointing and saying, "Here's the kitchen. Upstairs are three bedrooms." I had to stop him. It was making me sick. "This is your pitch? This is you selling the house?" He went quiet.

"Sell the house!" I barked. I almost felt bad, but it for his own good. "Do it again." He started up, providing a little more detail in a flat voice. "No. Do it again! Get excited! Sell! Tell me what's so great about this house!" He didn't know what to do. The poor guy was turning red.

The point is, anyone can lead a house tour. You need to sell the house and sell it like you live there and love it. It's your dream home. It's the best place you've ever seen. Find the unique points. Get excited. Read the client. Play up what they like, what they want, what they can't live without – this awesome house.

Last but not least, and by now I shouldn't even have to say this. Get contact info. Make sure to give and get cards. Have a sign-in sheet. Whatever. Exchange information, cell phone numbers, email addresses, compliments if you have to, but build your database. Then follow-up. Open. Work. Close. Stay in touch for future business with everyone. Everyone!

BROKER'S OPENS

Open houses for the trade – otherwise known as broker's opens or broker's caravans – are the best way to get other agents into your listings, checking out those properties for *their* buyers. You want to sell them. You want them to see the vision you have. You want them to be as excited about making money on these listings as you are: through the roof, passionate. Ready to close. This house won't be here tomorrow.

You want those magic words right from their mouth: "I have a client in mind." Damn right they do. They want to get paid.

At this point you gently squeeze them for all the information, all the leverage you can get on them and their clients. You're already sizing them up for negotiation. You have been, since advertising the open house, before they even walked in, but we'll get to more on that later.

Tell them about your other listings. They want you to. They need you to. Partner up. Create working alliances. Create buzz. Create as much potential new business as possible. Don't waste a moment.

Matt and I kill it with other agents. We already have a good cop/bad cop thing going on between us – me the aggressor, Matt holding the client's hand on the emotional rollercoaster of real estate. Adding another agent to the mix only amps that up. Working with sellers and buyers, depending on the temperament of the client, we need reinforcements. We bring in a new agent to back up our opinions on pricing, timing, and strategy.

With the above in mind, all agents should make it their business to visit open houses, especially broker's opens, regularly. Yours. Theirs. Whatever. You both have the same interest in mind. If not, then their client should be your client. Besides, how else are you going to learn what's out there?

And you need great houses to show. Even the duds can fill the gaps while you rush to find the golden properties. You need options to offer.

You need other agents to get excited about you walking into the room. You need contacts, clients, and closes. If a committed buyer shows up, you're ready. You're prepared. Open to close.

If you, the listing agent, set up an open house, pay for marketing, and advertise and produce the event, then you'll want a return on investment (ROI). There are many ways you can make this more profitable for yourself than for other agents, but this should be one of the easier parts of the job. You both want to make money, contacts, and future business.

Sell the house at every opportunity. Interact with all other agents. Interact with all potential clients. You may open a potential sale on a completely different listing. Get feedback on the price. Listen to comments about the property's strengths and weaknesses.

Always keep learning. If you assign the task to another agent, drop by. A real-deal, successful real estate CEO may drop in on up to 15 open houses a day. Nothing replaces that. On the days I'm not working one, I try to see at least 5 if not 15 more. If you're too much of a big shot, you're in the wrong line of work. I'll take your client. I'll take your money. I'll make deals with everyone else. Where the hell were you? Expand your reach.

INSIDER OPENS AND STRATEGIC ALLIANCES

Insider opens make me money. I love them, plain and simple. These events are targeted to those members of the real estate industry who could become players on your Dream Team. At the very least, these are industry professionals to network.

You'll bring them business. They'll bring you business. Giving to get. I'm talking developers, builders, and architects. I'm talking flippers, interior designers, and stagers. You want them to know you and you want to know them. You want them referring you to clients as well as asking you to represent their new constructions, renovations, and flips.

I already introduced you informally to the Josh Altman Dream Team of Closers and I refer business to them all the time just as they bring it to me. That's strategic alliance. Are you catching on yet? Insider opens make money.

Many times in this game a strategic alliance dictates my moves. I need to hook up a developer and build my reputation with them to get ongoing business. I'll take an overpriced listing with my eye on the long game, trying to land an ongoing business relationship. One of my favorite developers is a balls-to-the-wall, over-the-top, risk-loving old rocker. Another is a sophisticated European money guy who has a commercial real estate portfolio that includes buildings all over the world. Their work styles are wildly different but I'm cool with both of them, and they love real estate as much as me.

A guy I know does a $500 million a year in sales and $200 million of it is with the same developer. That's what ongoing relationships can do for your business. If you can't find any developers at the insider's open, then find construction sites where you're selling. Pull over the car and go walk the site. Ask who the developer is and where they are located. I talk to whomever I can find. I try to get something started. I make money.

It's the same with real estate investors. Didn't find any at the insider's open? Go where the money is and hang out with mortgage brokers. Since I was once one of those, I know lots of them, and we do a lot of recommending back and forth. Whatever market you sell, it's your job to meet mortgage brokers and they need to meet you. Offer advice. Ask for theirs. Trade secrets. Collaborate. Reach out. Meet them for coffee. Matt and I have done more than 1,000 deals in Los Angeles. About half of them were with developers and investors.

Whether it's broker's open or and insider's open, you are meant to be a networking hub for all your professional contacts. Know this. Breathe this. Give and receive. You're a middleman. You bring people together to make money. An insider's open can rocket that. You are LAX. You are Heathrow. You direct work to others and ask them to direct it to you. Throw wide.

And one more time: Give anyone and everyone your business cards and ask them to spread them to the usual suspects, and the unexpected ones, too. Get the contact info. Follow-up. This will lead to opens. Opens lead to close. You make money. Enough said.

Chapter 10

CREATE AN IN-YOUR-FACE BRAND, 24/7

You're now known. You've worked the open houses. You've shaken the hands, stats forward. You've built the database of contacts. You've sent follow-up emails. You started a monthly newsletter. Other agents, potential clients, developers, and industry professionals have met you. But do they really know you? Are you fully linked in their minds with what you sell? Or are you still just another agent in the game, the nice guy from an open house a few weeks ago?

Get in their face. Stay in their face. Show them who you are all the time.

Matt and I are not just rock stars in this game because of our stats. We're killing it even more because we are the face of luxury real estate. We are synonymous with high-end, multimillion-dollar dream living. We are the Nike sign of Los Angeles mansions, true ballers. Our brand is baller. We make it that way.

How have we accomplished this? We sell *ourselves* as much as we sell luxury property. We are old-school hand shakers, 100% accessible for our clients 24/7 in ways other agents avoid. We hit people over the head relentlessly with an image of success that marks us as experts, as ballers; we use numbers, follow-up emails, and newsletters to show off our "inventory": the best celebrity homes in Los Angeles.

But being on television has helped established us even more so, branding us in people's mind as the super-agents to the stars. It's been huge. And yet celebrity clientele may not watch the show. They know who we are because they themselves are big dogs. Nevertheless, our success and our presence on BRAVO act only as passive opens.

What we do next is take action to make ourselves visible at the highest end associated with our brand. Then, when someone goes digging, when someone thinks "I want a killer mansion overlooking the Pacific, there may be a few agents to go to, let me check out these LA TV guys, the Altman Brothers," we are ready to wow. Matt and I leave no question that we are boss, the guys to go to if you're licking your lips for luxury in Los Angeles.

WORKING THE WEB: SOCIAL MEDIA AND THE PRESS

Check out our website. What do you see? That's right, the dream. Visuals that say: "You've made it. You're Hollywood." A Rolls-Royce pulls into a circular driveway. There's a fountain in the center. The video pans to exclusive listing after exclusive listing. Infinity pools spill into the Pacific. Media rooms. Chef's kitchens. Putting greens. Windows floor to ceiling. Terrace fireplaces. Modern mansion after modern mansion from the canyons to the coast.

People now know our brand is baller because we put it in their face without doubt. We dress our business the same way we dress ourselves, sharp, expensive. The most modern technology allows state-of-the-art selling to further enhance the Altman brand.

For instance, we don't shoot videos for our website with iPhones. For us, cutting-edge technology is a huge open. The Altman Brothers are known for how we use tech. We hire an *Architectural Digest*–level photographer for every listing we represent, we make a "walk-through" 360-degree video of the interior, and we hire a drone team to film the outside.

By the time we've left the driveway, we have the listing. We've wowed a client and for a moment, we've gotten to feel like a kid again with a new toy. To get the listing we've taken the passive open of an internet video and flipped it into an active open with a hands-on demonstration.

Use everything you've got to open, work, and close. We've just renewed the drone contract for 50 flights. That's how killer it's been. It's our brand and it's in your face the moment you land on our site. Featured listings might come and go off thealtmanbrothers.com, but our milestone sales are always there, inviting potential clients to see our stats.

The combo of video and stills create movement and a sense of energy. Video also has stronger pull on Google rankings as does generating new content from blogs, Facebook, Instagram, and Twitter. This is another reason why you should spend the extra time each day posting, to drive whatever site you are connected to higher in the listings.

The giant websites – Trulia, Zillow, and Redfin – cover real estate for a massive worldwide audience. If you flow content through a website or blog, find a gap, an under-reported niche, something that means you specialize in areas – local or worldwide – that others do not. You're an expert. You're the go-to guy for certain desires. We are luxury LA. So, we put that out there.

Write about the issues common to your clients as they buy and sell real estate. Do you sell a lot of vacation properties? Are you in the mountains or by the sea? Selling barrier islands off the Carolina coast requires a different set of skills. You have them, others don't. Put that out there. If you've got specialized knowledge and experience, show it off. Everybody loves experts. Put it on your site. Post it online. Your brand needs to be repeated everywhere you appear.

Our "we sell the dream" branding is reinforced by text and image. So I won't be posting a selfie of me food shopping, but I will post a photo of Heather and me on the ramp of a private jet at LAX. My clients relate to that. They have private jet money (PJM). And if they want a house that screams they have it, then they know to call us.

Whether you drive a Camry down I-95 or cross the continent in a G650, pick the one your clientele can relate to and post it. That's what I mean by always thinking about branding.

To help us with all this, the Altman Brothers use consultants for internet marketing and publicity. Both fields change so quickly and are essential for making money. We want the best experts to do what they do, and we'll stick to the real estate. That's what we do.

Search engine optimization (SEO), hash tags, images, linking, video, and cross posting are all internet strategies that keep people on our site, clicking. The internet amplifies publicity, re-posting media across our social media platforms and pulling eyes toward our site, toward us, the closers. With a click or two a potential client is on our landing page, blown away, hungry, jealous, dreaming of success.

Get on Zillow. Your site's traffic will blow up as soon as you connect. Beware of trolls but overall, Zillow boosts your business energy and the good far outweighs any threats of strange posts.

Beyond a website, create a business page on Google. Link this page to your website, blog, twitter, Facebook, Instagram, YouTube, and so on to maximize SEO and drag your business up to a higher listing spot on the screen. Host webinars or teach a free class in real estate. Film it. Post it. Keep your feeds active.

Always provide your contact info and your website in anything you post. Let people know how to find you. That's the whole point. Never engage with anyone who wants to fight online. They're fools. They'll bring you down. Ignore them. Hide negative comments or turn them off completely and just broadcast. Don't be a schmuck.

The idea is to get people to stay on your site. You want to stay in their face all of the time. You want their jaws dropped in awe of what you offer, your brand. The longer they stay, the more chances you'll have to open, work, close. You'll make money. New content and images do this. Keep them flowing onto the page.

GIVE EXPERT ADVICE

Give advice as well. This keeps clients interested. Give to get. We have a section of our web presence dedicated to selling your home and what to look for when buying. This shares our expertise. We're giving to get. We're educating about the process that makes our jobs easier. As a result, people look to us as experts. When that happens, the press looks to us for comments. We love that. This "expert" role is also hugely useful to the press. More give to get. Once they see how open, smart, and easy you are to talk to, you'll hear from them on a regular basis.

Broker's caravans (opens) and other industry gatherings are a great place to meet real estate journalists. As you establish contacts, stay in their face. Forward them interesting information, insider tips and real estate gossip. Cultivate them as your "influencers," people who are highly visible and likely to mention your name on social media or among your professional peers. They'll market and brand for you. The result? PJM—private jet money.

These tactics will also lead to more money through speaking engagements. I speak all over the world and mentor young agents. I do this in part to pay it forward, and part for branding – more ways to open means more deals to close. For every person in the room, two more hear about the speech when they tell their friends. I give a talk to 3,000 people, who post about it on social media. The video goes up on YouTube and Facebook and thousands more see it. The word gets out.

A year ago I gave a speech in San Francisco. Afterward, Matt and I talked with this great guy and sent him some referrals. He didn't forget us. How could he? We were in his face, and because of our follow-ups and branding, we stayed in his face. When he encountered an overseas businessman's real estate agent who was searching in LA for his client, he referred the agent to us. Of course, we took the lead. We always take the lead.

The listing we had to show was known as the "White House of the West," Dorothy Chandler's house, as in Dorothy Chandler Pavilion, home of the Academy Awards for many years. We had it on the market for $10 million. The place actually did resemble the White House slightly, with a long winding front walk to where huge columns form a portico. Eisenhower, Kennedy, Johnson, and Nixon had all slept in this American Beaux-Arts house designed by the three architects who created Hearst Castle.

I mean this home was historic and baller, sitting right on Windsor Square in Hancock Park. Neighbors once included J. Paul Getty and now the mayor of Los Angeles. The house has undergone five massive renovations and has 400-year-old French limestone on the kitchen floors, a new swimming pool with an Ozone system, a music room with a grand concert piano, a new irrigation system, and a new landscaping design. The overseas businessman and his agent walked the house and said they'd take it. Just like that. Matt and I shot each other a look, said our farewells and kept moving.

The next morning, boom, $10 million was wired into escrow ! I wish it could always be that easy. That was a good day in real estate and all because through branding I opened myself up to speaking engagements as a form of more branding, a form of marketing, a form of opening to close.

To keep going with this mindset of branding, the Altman Brothers recently leased new office space in Beverly Hills, the old Lululemon storefront. We needed more room because we're killing it, yes, but truly the move was strategic in that location for more in-your-face branding. We are a fabric of the neighborhood, the face of success. We have large windows in the front, where we'll set up a weekly podcast with celebrities and real estate stars that we'll then promote from our social media feeds. It's in your face in the richest neighborhood in the nation.

Is Beverly Hills really the richest neighborhood in the nation? It doesn't matter. It's associated as such. It's branded. It's Beverly Hills. That's us: the Altman Brothers for all to see. We are this neighborhood; we represent this neighborhood. We buy, sell, and build this neighborhood. We're baller.

Who are you? Are you even an agent? If I go to your website right now will you be proud of what I find? Can I find you anywhere online? If I can, will I know immediately what it is that you offer, that you sell? Will this make me trust you as a closer? Are you who I want to work with? Do you scream success?

CONCIERGE EXTRAORDINAIRE

You're going "Hollywood" now, which means that above and beyond your brand, you need to up what you offer. There's an advanced Game-Time mentality you as an agent need to understand, that you need to possess if you want to make money like we make money. Ready for it?

You don't just sell houses. You sell lifestyle. You sell dreams. You sell the unattainable and you make it easy for your client to get. To do this, you're prepared to offer your client anything. As long as it's legal, you answer the phone and you make it happen. Otherwise – and this is especially true with the superstar clientele we have – they'll just call someone else. And when it comes time for an investment property, they'll call that person again instead of you.

You're "Hollywood" now, so you need to become a concierge. Here's the deal.

Matt just heard from a client we sold a house for (and to) last year. He called because he now wants a playground in his yard. Do you think we at the Altman Brothers were like, "Sorry, bro, we sell houses, not slides and swingsets"? Hell no! Matt smiled and responded, "No problem."

Within the hour he found a company that manufactures and constructs playgrounds, sent over brochures to the client, and then orchestrated a purchase and installation. Matt closed. No commission check – but remember, this is the long play. That client will eventually be in the market for a new home, or know others who are, and will call *us*. Why? Because we get things done. Whatever's needed.

This all ties in with Robert Cialdini and his restaurant/mint experiment. Give to get. We act like a concierge to the rich as much as we act like their real estate agent. Nothing beats personal service and that is what we provide at top level. Our clients know that we've got their backs no matter what.

Need a pool guy? No problem. Lakers tickets? No problem. Lawn care? No problem. Yacht rental? Done. Oh, you want to look at houses in the middle of the night because can't miss the concert at the Hollywood Bowl first, and then you're going to hit a few nightclubs? We got VIP passes. Our car will get you at the airport. Where would you like to go to dinner? Boom. Business. Long-term.

We get requests for anything and everything and we always rise to the challenge. We are the best. You can be too. Please your clients. Open, work, close. Do this and you too will make money.

Chapter 11

GOLDEN HAMMERS AND 20 QUESTIONS FOR SELLERS

Y ou've got your head in the game, ready to serve your clients in all ways: prepared to please, and ready to open, work, and close. Your brand game and in-your-face strategy is strong. So what's the next thing you – a new agent now, all "Hollywood" – need to consider as you prep yourself for meeting buyers and sellers in the walk-through?

SHUT UP AND LISTEN

The first thing you should pay attention to is your mouth – the best and worst thing you have going for you. Your mouth can both earn and cost you money, like mine has done for me. I mentioned this earlier when I talked about first appearances, but here it's a matter of allowing the information to get to you before you piss off the person giving it – the potential client.

You want to be a great closer? Listen up. Seriously, in general, listen. Real estate is constant negotiation, and the more information you have – the more understanding of the motivations of all parties – the more effective you'll be in getting the best deal. You can't shut up enough if you want a killer close. Either you're a beast or you're not, but even beasts have to hold their tongue, open their ears, and pay attention.

Microsoft oversaw recent testing of the attention span of today's average person. Scientists studied 2,000 people and the EEGs (electroencephalograms) of 112 more and found that, since the year 2000 to the present day, the human brain has dropped its ability to hold focus from 12 seconds to 8 seconds. That's right, 8 seconds! This means buyers' minds are wandering before you even get through the foyer. If you have so little time, talk fast. I don't mean blurt it out, cutting people off. I mean start with the most important strategy, or selling points. Focus the client, then shut up and listen.

Mastering that aspect of real estate time had a huge impact on my closes. If I didn't hang onto the potential client's words, I missed too much that's important for leverage during the close. Even worse, I pissed people off. Do that and there's no deal.

In the early days of the Altman Brothers, Matt and I were walking a house with an elderly seller. As she was taking us through her home I was already crunching numbers, fully aware that the place was a shithole. Matt, being Matt, was cued into the seller and her relationship with the house. As we went through rooms, she said thing like "here is where my daughter got married" and "this basement has seen its share of slumber parties." I heard her, but I wasn't really listening. I was in my head, already deciding it all. At the end of the tour, she asked us what we thought. Matt opened his mouth to speak, but I beat him to it.

"This house is a complete tear-down."

The woman snapped. I mean she was heated. She grabbed us both by the collars and yelled, "Get out!" Then she pulled and pushed us through the front door, her bony hands around my neck like in a horror movie. I was so shocked all I could do was laugh. Matt and I ran down the front walk to the car, fleeing before she pulled out a shotgun or came out after us with a knife. She was mad.

Inside the car, Matt exploded, "What the hell is the matter with you?!" I was laughing so hard I couldn't look at him. Matt understood the emotions of real estate long before I did. The woman loved her home. It was her baby, and I had just suggested we destroy it. Why? Because instead of listening, I was in my head making moves as if she viewed the selling as a business deal. What I should have been doing was listening, searching for the "golden hammer."

The "golden hammer," as we like to call it, is the detail or tool that gives you the leverage you'll use in negotiations. You have to listen to get all the details and you have to quickly sift through those details to find the golden hammer. Golden hammers can range from the knowledge that the sellers are getting divorced to withering assessments such as "the pool looks like it was dug in the 1940s." Golden hammers are the issues – small and big – that you use to beat the hell out of your opponent. It's what you need most to get the best deal for your client.

We'll come back to it later and talk about how to use it best, but you need to know now that this is what you're looking for even before walking through the door. Keep track of your hammers as you work the deal, because you never know what you'll need for the close.

As you listen, look for a pause, a hesitation, a deflection, or a question left repeatedly unanswered. Usually if someone doesn't answer a question, there's something they don't want to talk about. They don't want to lose money. They don't want to give you the hammer.

This brings us to 20 Questions. We all know this game: You ask an opponent questions that must be answered with only a "yes" or a "no," then try to figure out their secret identity.

When I walk through potential listing, I'm on it. I'm asking 20 Questions, but I'm not really looking for a "yes" or "no" answer. I'm looking for deeper emotional responses. As you may remember with the old lady who tried to choke me out – and she really did try – real estate is about emotion, at least the first time around.

The rational mind will eventually show up, but you can't rush real estate. Let people pour their hearts out; you pay attention, look for the golden hammer, then become a killer negotiator for your client. I need a lot of answers in a short amount of time. In a perfect world, those answers come before the listing agreement is signed so we can cut right through the crap.

Listen, the point is to get the seller to sign, but it only helps you later to get all the details now. That way you know what tools you have to use when the final battle goes down. This is war. Details are your weapons. The gold hammer is your canon. If I learn my sellers are getting divorced, they might want an all-cash offer, even if the offer is lower, just to move on; that leaves an opening for a fast close.

If a buyer has to move into the city to begin work on September 1, they might spend more to get the kids here for the start of school; that means you might show a pricier listing. That's why you play 20 Questions. You're searching for your close.

Now, while Matt is busy holding the scorned divorcee's hand about selling the home in which she raised her kids, I am more likely crunching the numbers and figuring out all the angles. Still, we have two sets of questions, one for sellers and one for buyers. I change them up based on the situation, my instincts, and who is leading me through the house. I play the game as it goes. I smile. I hustle. I ask. I listen. I dig for the golden hammer. I open to close.

THE ALTMAN 20 (QUESTIONS FOR SELLERS)

1. **Why are you leaving such a beautiful house?**

   A little flattery and a bit of fishing for the truth about why they're leaving, and why now, will pay off. Too small? Too big? Kids? Relocation? Death? Divorce? I hate to say it, but a client's divorce can be an agent's friend. I usually can land two separate clients from one home. Just saying.

2. **When did you buy this house? Who from? Does the house have a story?**

   If the present owners built the house, the answers to these questions take a bit of time, but are usually worth it. A builder can tell you problems you would have never seen until inspection. Or, if there is cool, unique history behind the house, you can use it to target certain buyers it might appeal to.

3. **Do you have children? Did they like the house?**

   Kids are a huge driver for families. Is the house kid-friendly or a death trap? How many kids lived there, and who fit where? If it's an obvious bachelor pad I skip this one.

4. **What do you love about living here?**

   Listen hard here. People actually tell you what to use in your closing strategy. Steal it. Use it. Sell it. If the house has an eight-bay climate-controlled garage, I'm calling car collectors. What speaks to one owner about a house will usually speak to another.

5. **What would you change?**

   I used to say "what do you hate about this house?" and people got defensive. They are aware they are opening me to sell their house and they don't like to talk trash. So I've softened my approach, and the answer is something I can use to soften a buyer. It will be my "give to get," showing the potential buyer that I too see a small flaw, and I'm not working them over. I'm being honest.

6. **Did you entertain? Often? How?**

This is LA, of course there were parties! Find out what kind of entertaining went down in the house and you've got yourself a target on a style of buyer.

7. **Did you like the neighborhood?**

This one's huge. Listen carefully to what you hear and what you don't. Was this a good 'hood for the adults or the kids? Is it a trick-or-treat Halloween block? Bikes ever stolen? Were you in walking distance to the park, the bar, the market?

8. **How are your neighbors?**

I make good use of responses like "the dude across the street turns into a rowdy Philly Eagles fan every Sunday," or "I've never met a one of them" during showings.

9. **How did you use the outdoor space?**

In my market, backyards most often have infinity pools and spectacular landscaping. These features may not be the right fit for everyone, but details about how a family used these premiums – or didn't – can make great talking points and add big to the final price of the property.

10. **Have you updated the kitchen during your time here? Did you replace any appliances? Backsplash? Counters? Sinks? Floors? How long ago?**

Kitchens are a flashpoint. New appliances and a working island with eat-in capability are essential in my market. What's essential in the kitchens in your market? If there's updating to be done, warn the seller it may come off the list price, setting up that for conversation later.

Otherwise, ask about any "green" updating – solar-generated energy, water-saving appliances, saltwater pools, or sustainable materials. Younger buyers love that stuff, especially in LA. Have your Dream Team contractors in mind to recommend, should they make any updates to the property.

11. **Let's talk bathrooms. Have you renovated lately?**

Bathrooms are another flashpoint. From my point of view, you can't have a master bath big enough; it's good for marriage.

Whirlpool tubs, double vanities, steam showers, double rain show-
erheads, heated floors, and lots of storage are high on "want" lists.
Stay on trends and accentuate any positive aspect about bathrooms;
beautiful bathrooms sell houses. And again, remember your Dream
Team.

12. **What parts of the house did you spend the most time in?**

Usually, I hear kitchen, bedrooms, and media or family room.
Isn't life about food, sleep, and TV? Sometimes I get a unique
response that gives me a style of buyer to hunt out.

A couple years back I sold a house where one floor had been
converted to a recording studio. My colleague brought in his
client, a young songwriter with wealthy parents, to see the house.
It was perfect; she loved it. I used this as leverage and got the other
agent up during final negotiations. Where else would she find a
ready-built studio designed and built by a famous musician? I was
pumped.

13. **Do you have security systems working? Have you installed CCTV
cameras? Is there direct street access to the front door? Are there
sight lines from the street?**

I work with famous wealthy people whose jobs come with safety
concerns. They have stalkers. It's crazy. Sure they can afford to wire
a house and put in front gates, but if I can use security details during
a showing, I want to know. No celebrities enjoy a tour bus pulling
up as they take out the trash. Know security coverage and the neighborhood's crime report.

14. **What were your commutes like?**

This is a huge quality-of-life question in most American cities.
My clients don't have as many issues with commuting. They run
the company, are on tour, or are making films. But most buyers do;
on average, this is a hot button and you need a sense of where you
are. If the house is an hour from the city's center, it'll be tough selling it to someone on a tight clock. Know your client's life, whether
buying or selling. Then play on what they need.

15. **May I walk around the house outside?**

Curb appeal is huge. So is easy access around the property. If you
find tilting brick walls or imploded garden sheds, you know what to
do – leverage on pricing and remember your Dream Team. Yards
and outdoor spaces matter; UK's *The Guardian* found that a garden
added 20% to the final price of houses. The Brits have always loved

their gardens, but now Americans have gone nuts for the natural world. Southern California has always done the indoor/outdoor living thing really well, and my clients expect it.

16. **What did you pay for the house? What price would you like to list?**

    This is a loaded question with an often-laughable answer: The first part of the question is public information; any self-respecting agent already knows the last sale price coming in it, and knows it will have a huge impact on the list price and negotiations. If your seller overpaid, the next buyer's agent should know that, and counter the price accordingly.

    If the seller wants to overprice, tell them your concerns. If you don't speak up, the client will blame you completely if the house fails to sell. Although a firm pricing agreement is not required now, this is a good time to plant a seed in your client's mind about pricing. More on this in a bit.

17. **Can we talk about timing?**

    In my sellers' market, houses fly. They change hands overnight. Some clients prefer pocket (exclusive) listings because they are unadvertised. They want it before it goes on sale. They want privacy. Negotiate the length of the agreement now; only you can assess the amount of both time and money you'll invest to sell the property. More on this, too, in a bit.

18. **Will we be able to show the house when we need to?**

    From the door, emphasize to your potential clients that the more they make the house available for you to work, the faster you can close. Reinforce the "team" element of your work. They need to trust you. You can't sell a house you can't show.

19. **If I end up representing you, how would you like to communicate? Phone, text, email?**

    We're available 24/7 for our clients, but the client doesn't always share the same motto. That can get tricky with showings. Still, as an agent it's a must. Never leave a client hanging. Success in real estate is 90% about communicating with and managing your client: You avoid misunderstandings by staying in touch.

    I remember a season or two ago on the show, my colleague had a developer's listing and I jacked it because he hadn't called the guy in months with an update. Don't go quiet because you have no offers to report. I have never had a client say, "don't call me so much." Every week call your active opens, or call a few of them every morning before you hit the street. Send a quick text or email.

Just do this and you'll see your stock rise. Clients love feedback. They need to trust you. If you have nothing to tell, still don't leave them hanging. Walk into the punch. Take the hit. Get it over with. It beats the alternative – losing them.

20. **And here's the pitch:**

We whip out our stats. They speak for themselves. We preach our availability, 24/7, unlike no other agent. We've got your back, any time, any day. We let the seller know they are the coach. They call the plays. We'll give it all we have. We'll make money. We mean it and we do.

Chapter 12

SIZE UP THE PROPERTY: PRICING AND TIMING

Let's say a potential client (a seller) has already given me (the rock-star, baller agent) the once-over. I've done the same to them. That's the human side of the equation, with all the factors that can make us a good fit. But let's forget about people for a second and focus on the bricks and mortar. Let's look at the house itself – and see how I size that up.

Do I like it? Do I want it on my team? The answer is most often yes, since Matt and I don't leave money on the table. We make money. We take risk. We accept challenge. We win games. Let's play.

Beyond the owner, the other most valuable asset, what do I see? What do I like? Do I want to represent this? Is this my brand? Is this worth my time? How could I position this home for the market? How could I make this work?

READING THE PROPERTY: QUESTIONS I ASK MYSELF

Is this a good house from a real estate agent's point of view? Will it be easy to sell?

Don't shy away when the answer is no. Get creative.

Will this property require a specific buyer? Who do I have in mind?

Ask the right questions. One man's trash is another man's treasure. Think like others even outside of your standard client base. Who can I reach?

Does my experience tell me it will be difficult to find a buyer for this home?

Size it up properly. Compare it with your previous sales. What can you learn from those to help sell this one? How can you solve the difficulty?

Do I understand the house and how people live in it?

What works? What doesn't? What plays to family, to singles, to the elderly?

What houses have sold in this neighborhood in the last six months?

Do your research. Be prepared. Check your comps – all of them. Get ready to point them out.

What is happening in the neighborhood? Construction? Crime? School zone? Proximity?

What's it smell like in the morning here? What's it sound like outside for now? What about later? Is it safe? Can kids ride their bikes? What can I walk to quickly? Stores? The beach? A park? The highway? Target your clients accordingly.

How are the neighboring houses like or unlike this one? Style? Condition? Privacy? Outdoor space?

Does this design fit the neighborhood? Is this out of place or unique? Is the property tucked away or does it stand out? Use this knowledge.

Does the home need updating? How much? How willing is the owner to do it? What developers do I know who are willing to get their hands dirty? Anyone on my Dream Team?

What can go and what can stay? Any easy fixes? Know the prices. Know the options. Have the suggestions.

Is this a motivated seller? Or no? Ah, there I go again. I just grouped seller with property? Is that not the job?

Yes, it is the job. How much will they get in their own way? Can you massage that? How?

What are the utilities like? Is this a monster to run from month to month?

Know the client's money and care. Research. Ask. Listen. Do the math. Present reality.

Is this a rehab? Is this a tear-down? What will the seller be open to? I'm listening, hunting for the hammers. Are they there?

Be ready to recommend options with value assessed. Think of alliances that could benefit all. Let them know what they hadn't considered is actually a great deal. Be respectful. Be sensitive.

What about building code? Permits? Height restrictions? Laws?

One thing a lot of agents overlook is the basic details of how a new owner can legally change a property. The good agents have this covered.

But even more worrisome – especially when you're dealing with a buyer – is being ignorant of how a neighbor who alters or does construction to their property may affect the listing at hand. Many agents shy away from this for a reason. They don't want to turn off their client. Know the laws. Know the rules. It can be used as leverage.

Once, and only once, were Matt and I blindsided by this. We had a property in the Hills. It was a new construction property. We took the listing. The owners of the house that went up behind our listing sued the owners of my listing because it was 2 feet higher than the building code. We couldn't give that house away and, as far as I know, it's still locked in legal hell. In plain, it sucked. We spent thousands on an unsellable house. Beware.

This happens all over in all ways. In New York, residents sue builders over the shadows their skyscrapers cast. Become familiar with the building permits in your area. City governments post all building permits online, and they are accessible to anybody. We were mad at ourselves on that one.

Finally, is this property a winner or a pig? How can I work with a pig?

Who do I know? What do I know? How can I spin it? I think about this: all of it; every aspect. I take these factors into every consideration. I'm a killer and I often never say no unless it comes down to ridiculous pricing. So, eventually, I arrive at pricing. The price will determine my timeframe, and the timeframe may determine my price. The price will lead me to who, what, where, and how.

LET'S TALK PRICING

The more you know, the better. Research the hell out of the house. Find out when it changed hands and for how much. Figure out the comps' average price per square foot. Compare listing prices (first asking price) to sales price ratio (actual selling price) for the neighborhood comps in the last six months, if possible. You will rely on what the comparative market analysis (CMA) tells you over and over again. It's the foundation of your strategy.

I've been doing this a long time. In my market, I do a lot this stuff in my head. As I drive to meet the seller and see the house, I'm thinking, I sold a house on this block two years ago for $6 million: same view, same east-west orientation, same number of bedrooms, same-sized pool. I've got a number in my head but when I arrive, I see the view is partially obstructed. There's a lot of noisy construction on the street and the exterior looks cheap. That's when the $6 million in my head starts deflating. There's just no getting around reality, no matter how much buzz and how many pictures you post. A seller knows what they paid for their house, and they want to make a profit. So, I go to work. I have to adjust expectations of the seller.

Owners tend to value their house higher than the market because they want to make money, and they made a lifetime of memories while living there. The challenge here is to get the listing and get the seller to set the right price. If I let an unreasonable client list a property that's not been renovated in a decade for 20% over market, in most markets I'll fail. Negotiate on price with your client. Know the money. Do the math.

Put the carrying costs and timing in their face versus the crafted drop in price. The listing battle is the first war of selling the property. No matter how long your contract runs, overpriced houses don't often move easily, even in my fierce market. As soon as you get the listing price where it should have been in the beginning, boom! It sells. Handle the client from the door, and set yourself up right for your close.

Don't be a "yes man" when it comes to price. It's been easier for Matt and me to avoid being that person as our business has grown and proven our stats. Clients argue less with us because we're experts at this and they know it. Check our brand. Still, you get the egos, the wannabe pros. I am amazed at how many people call me – experts in acting, directing, music, technology, and finance – to argue about some negotiation or another. I always say the same thing: "I've been doing this for a long time. I'd take your opinion on who has the best recording studio in LA, so why won't you take advice on real estate?" This can be even harder when dealing with developers.

In one nightmare situation my client and her mother were locked in a war fighting over everything including the pricing. Worse, what they didn't do was pay the mortgage for two years. I lost a potential commission on $6.75 million when the listing went into foreclosure. I was ripped.

Then, to add injury to insult, I get a call from a developer who bought the house at the bank auction. He's putting $2 million into it and wants to put it on the market. Would I sell it? I wanted to recoup the time and energy I spent on this listing, but once burned, I hesitated. This listing felt like real estate dark matter; everybody that came near it was sucked into the void.

I asked him how much he wanted to list for and when he said his number, I laughed. I said, "List it at $11,995,000, you'll get ten to ten and a half, recoup your investment and make another $2 million after that." He thanked me politely and we hung up. A year later – and four years after I first saw this house – the guy calls me back. The listing didn't move at his price of $13,995,000 and he was willing to try mine. We dropped it to $11,995,000; it sold, and I finally made a commission. You can't make people take your number, but you can insist on not taking theirs. Again, pricing, and in final negotiations, are often the only times we say no.

Assess the house. If there's a logical reason to put the house on the market for a higher price, do it. If not, you set up to fail. Even if the client insists, warn them. You'll still get blamed, but warn them.

You may have your reasons for wanting the listing anyway. It could be a prestigious seller who opens you up to a whole new set of potential opens. It could be great press coverage. You may want to work with this particular developer. If you want the listing and take it at an inflated price, you'd better warn them with proof before agreement.

Do your research and smash your data: square feet, comps, number of bedrooms, bathrooms, most recent renovations, and so on. Have a price range in mind and back it up. Bring visual aids to the listing appointment if you must. Put the comps in their face. Warning the seller is all.

I take listings that the seller lists too high all the time, but I always insist on the right number prior to signing and continue to press my case for dropping the price if the property doesn't sell. It's the job. An Altman technique we use is to ask the client to write what they think their house will sell for on a piece of paper and we write what we think it will sell for on a separate piece of paper. After three months on the market with no sale yet, we open our estimates. We don't shame them too much, but we do smile. This diffuses anger. This affirms expertise. This gets repeat business. We know what we're doing. We make money.

One angle to play in super-hot markets is purposely underpricing, knowing they will get multiple offers that drive the final number up. Another angle is to agree to price high, but get an assurance from your seller to reassess and drop the price every 30 days. Also, always follow the "Rule of 99" – it's a $1,499,000 house, not a $1,500,000 house. Come on.

I'm in the middle of working a close for a client who doesn't understand why the house isn't worth more. Eight years ago the house was an awesome cutting-edge design, but modern goes out of style quicker than anything. She wouldn't budge, and we wanted the listings to start working that section of town due to the presence of certain developers. So, after five or six months, we brought in another agent to co-list with us and back us up on price. Another professional voice in her ear was what we needed to sway her. We sold the house. Our commission was split, yes, but we now work the hell out of that neighborhood.

On the flip side, I watch the overpriced listings of others like a hawk. These are perfect deals to grab from the first or second agent. That's what I mean when I say I watch listings. They are not just proof to your overpricing client, but it's an open in someone else's failing close. Pay attention. You're hunting – food for your client and another agent's lunch. They should have been able to work it. They didn't. We take it. Then, we put the facts of this in our original overpricing clients' face. They can't argue. They'll try, but they can't. Now we've got a win-win. It's all about the pricing. Set up to close.

Pricing of course, leads me to timing. As mentioned above, I'll use the threat of time versus carrying costs as a weapon in negotiating pricing with the client. Agents must also consider the timing for themselves. Is it worth it? Again, we don't often say no to a listing, but is this a winning listing? Does the shot clock at play allow it to succeed? Is this filler for me, just something to gamble on, offer as an option to others until I find another gold star? What's my timeframe? What's the client's timeframe? What's the market's timeframe? How does this affect the pricing?

Keep in mind that once you sign that listing, your first month will be spent on open houses, showings, then finalizing and executing your marketing plan. It's "feedback" month. What you hear now will drive your pitch as you work the sale hard. In a cold or buyer's market, six months should be the shortest. In rural areas, a year is reasonable. If the seller is leaving the country for two months and doesn't want the house shown, find that out now.

The longest listing Matt and I ever worked was an awesome house in the Bird Streets in my Hollywood Hills, and for whatever reasons we couldn't sell it. It took a year and seven months. The client was loyal, a rare thing in our market. He didn't fire us when listing agreement after listing agreement came up for renewal. Finally, we brought on another agent to change the energy, as we'll do with overpricing, and change it he did.

We sold the house to another Altman Brothers client, a marijuana king. How another agent brought us to our own client, we're not sure, but the clients are happy and we made money. I guess it was all in the timing. That said, when the numbers don't add up, the score is tied, overtime is reached, and you're at stalemate, go with your gut. Remember, you're "Hollywood" now.

Chapter 13

CLOSE THE OPEN
ON SELLERS: TALK
MARKETING, THEN SIGN

At this point in my career I often land a listing to sell on my presence alone. But there was a time when this required more of a fight for Matt and me.

Still, the game for certain A-list clients and multimillion-dollar developers is always to test you. They want their team leaders on their toes at all times. Keep 'em sharp. No matter the position of your career or the listing and client you're trying to land, there are a few tricks you always can use.

As I've said, the first thing I push is my availability and willingness to hustle. I make sure the client knows this, and that no one else will measure up to me. No one will be there to fight for a client with as much force and speed as I will. That's the way I have branded our business: 24/7 for you.

The next thing is, through research and gut instinct we know that people respond differently to different people. So the Altman Brothers will often close an open as a pair, a team. We often work together for listing appointments. A potential seller might like me and not Matt, or the other way around – Matt is often a shoulder to lean on while I aggressively bite my way through, ready to kill competition.

Recently my wife Heather and I met with a property manager who right away took to Heather's refined and amazing charm. My wife correctly believed she had the listing. We then met with the owner. Turns out he was an old numbers guy, a businessman. He preferred to do business with me, warming instead to my animal instinct. But we would have never gotten near him if it weren't for Heather's dynamic with the manager.

Another secret weapon is that I show the house before I get the listing. I go right to work. I'm on it from the door. I've even showed up with possible buyers to start if I know in good faith the potential client will be cool with it. I take two or three of my buyers through the property so the maybe-client can see how hard I will work for them. Of course, if my buyers like it, at best I double-end it and at the least, I've got some feedback to sell my active buyers' houses faster. Either way, the listing owner knows I don't play around, I play ball. I'm all business. I open. I work. I close. I make money.

Another wildcard I throw their way is the marketing budget. Pitch your thoughts on how you'll reach the house's market after the walk-through, straight and up front. Most sellers don't even consider our investment and the very mention of it lets them know you have skin in the game, too. Not only that, but using a technique suggested by Professor Cialdini's "mints for tips" experiment, we spend more to make more. This attracts potential clients to use us more.

For my luxury LA real estate listings, I invest marketing dollars at top industry standard – 10%. That's a growth number; others believe 5% is enough to keep their business moving at the same pace. That's cool for others, but I just don't stop there. The Altman Brothers go all out. Sell the possible client on the whole package – photography, video, MLS costs, print, internet advertisements, open house food and drink with a DJ. It's all part of the work and close that will come later, and key to landing the listing now. I let the client know that I make them part family, our brand, and they already know our brand is baller.

We think of our marketing budgets for listings as subsets of our brand marketing budgets, and we weave the listings into aspect of marketing we do. We also pull the Altman brand into listing advertisements, running our logo and stats on everything. It's a double play, a win-win. Everything feeds everything in marketing. It's how we get our money's worth, impress the client, and close the best possible deal.

Reinvest in your business by marketing your listings and you'll keep from leaving more money on the table. You'll fuel your brand. Give to get. Money makes money. We spend money. We give to get money. We make money.

Now it's time for the ink – signing the listing agreement. Anything can be negotiated here. No rules. Anything plays. National standards range from 5% in California to 6% in New York. This means that here in California I will take a 2.5% commission and the other agent gets the same.

The length of agreement is usually between six months to a year, the year being for rural and slower moving markets. The agreement can be renewed and renegotiated for as long as you and the client choose. Shoot for the six months, at least. In real estate time, you lose the first couple weeks to prepping the listing for market, so build time for launch into your agreement.

You can represent the listing with an "exclusive right to sell," meaning only you get access to the property. You can also sign an "exclusive agency listing" meaning anyone in your firm can show it. An "open listing" works just like it sounds, anyone can show the house.

Remember, there's no loyalty in real estate, so even the listing agreement is made to be broken. I've made millions of dollars for clients and that night I've seen them nestled at a corner table in Beverly Hills, a new agent whispering sweet nothings into their ear as I pass by, barely acknowledged. That's real estate. That's my game and now it's yours.

Chapter 14

CLOSE THE OPEN ON BUYERS: THE ALTMAN 12

W e roll out the red carpet when we're repping buyers. We please. We impress. We gain their confidence. We show them a good time. This is when Matt and I go beyond being real estate agents. This is the Altman Brothers all-exclusive concierge service. For a buyer, this is fun. I'd work with us if I were buying. This part's for us, too. Let it be fun for you as well.

What do we offer? Everything and anything as long as it's legal. Most importantly, we offer our clients luxury and privacy while touring listings. We provide access to the most exclusive events and impossible-to-book restaurant tables in the city. After all these years, Matt and I have massive reach within the real estate industry worldwide. Trust me.

If you're looking to buy with us as your agents, you're going to have a good time, no cameras in your face. LA becomes yours and if you let us do our job, sit back, and simply pick what you want, you'll be happily paying taxes in no time. You'll be a resident. You'll have a baller home. And you'll always have the Altman Brothers to call.

For buyers, I've cut the number of questions almost in half of the amount as sellers. Why? Endless data tells me buyers fall in love with a house in an instant; Kahneman's System 1 thinking takes hold first: You like what you like on the surface without the need for deliberation. My first objective is to figure out what makes a buyer smile. For some it's an entryway, for others a kitchen, for some a master suite or city view at night. Find "must haves" and walk directly toward those when touring a house.

But, as I tell my buyers, no matter what the house, act cool. Even if we've been back three times to look, a friendly, detached attitude works best. Believe me, if a seller's agent sees a buyer in love, then that becomes a huge weakness when trying to save that buyer money at the final negotiation table.

If I'm showing the house to my buyer and I see the look, I begin working on their System 2 thinking. I fill in the facts. I build the story. I focus on concerns about risk and error. Are they buying the right house? Will it appreciate? Will their family be happy here? Facts are the money, square footage, comps, taxes, and the neighborhood. The "story" of how they'll live in the house. Pay attention to this. Listen. You'll need a story to write for your client. Once the facts and the story come together, you make your move. You close.

Questions for the buyer are where all the dreams come into play. It's one thing for a person to leave a home, but to start something new gets exciting. This is the awesome journey of how a buyer wants to live. This is the new house. This is the new life. This is the upgrade, the vision within reach. This is the family castle. This is the buyer making the scene – Hollywood.

1. **Why do you want a new house?**

   Know why and when your client needs to be in a new house. This will aim you right at your first showings.

2. **What's your top price?**

   Question #1 will help you get a true idea of a price cap. Many buyers won't often be honest with this answer upfront. Challenge the budget if needed, being truthful about what that price will really get them. Be the reality check upfront. Back it up if need be. The client's first reality check is you. The second reality check is finding out what their money buys. The third check is losing a house they've made an offer on. Don't let them get there by not being straight up. Refine strategy if necessary.

3. **Cash versus financing?**

The majority of US real estate is financed. Research mortgages. Know all rates. In a seller's market, your client must be ready with money to offer at any time. Cash is speedier. No paperwork. To win, sometimes cash needs to be spent, prices need to be matched and beaten. Cash is king.

But either way, lock up houses with an offer if the buyer's in love. Don't be afraid to offer and counteroffer on multiple houses. In California, once in escrow on an average deal, the buyer has 10 to 20 days to figure it out. Order the inspections. If minds change, cancel the offer before contingencies expire. No explanation necessary. The buyers get their money back, except for inspection fees. I advise my clients to do this every time. It beats the alternative of losing out.

4. **Tell me about your family. What does your house need?**

How many rooms? Beds? Baths? Kitchen? Dining? Family room? Basement? Storage? You'll weed out most of the market listings here. And involve the kids. It's a fun time for all. Be part of the family. Get the details. Find what they need. Have fun.

5. **What do you want? What do your kids want? Dream scenario?**

Wants are different than needs. As I said in the 20 Questions for Sellers, kids have pull. Ask everybody what he or she wants. Consider this as the "what's your dream house" question. I hear "pool," "outdoor space," and "chef's kitchen" every time. This will direct your original search even more. Remember the clock. Remember the options. Remember your Dream Team can help get you there even if a little work needs to be done.

6. **What neighborhood? Why?**

It's often all about location. Find out why. If you know why they love a certain area, but can't find the right house, you can recommend similar neighborhoods. Never assume your buyer knows everything about the city you sell. They're the coach, but you're driving.

7. **Is commuting a factor?**

Be aware of commute times, highway proximity, and public transportation. Put them in the car and take the drive. Let them feel it. Commuting can be a serious issue. The staffing and management firm Robert Half did a survey of 1,800 workers nationwide and found that 23% had left their jobs because of a tortuous commute. It matters. A lot.

8. **Private or public schools?**

Know the schools. Know the school zones. Hell, know the curriculum. This will play into commutes, neighborhoods, needs, and wants.

9. **Do you entertain? How?**

Big family? Work functions? Barbeques and football Sundays? Holidays? Like to host? Like to party? Formal? Casual? How do you like to unwind? How and with whom do you celebrate? How a person entertains can outweigh location and other factors, open floor plan and flow, parking. It's often about the party. People like to entertain in their homes. It's about pride.

10. **Specific requests? Privacy? Gated? Guest rooms? Home offices? Recording studio? Smart houses? Energy-efficient houses? Huge garage? Infinity pool? Screening room? Ocean view?**

Listen, you've seen our website by now and you know our clientele. Everything is desired and anything is possible. People want their home customized to them and their lives. Finding homes that accommodate the client's dream will target your search and please more than anything. Get creative.

I've had an arms dealer in need of an underground bunker. I had requests for home surgery centers (plastic), hair salons, gyms, indoor basketball courts, bowling alleys, shooting ranges (underground in LA), growing facilities (pre–Proposition 64 vote), secret passages for a guy to sneak women out as others came in, hidden rooms for adult play, helicopter pads, and eight-car garages. Be ready for any type of request and if you can't find it, find the people who can build it.

11. **How do you want us to work with you? Do you like phone, text, or email?**

Because of the Altman Brother's concierge services, we have protocols for every client. We've had buyer meetings on film sets and in offices, grocery stores, pools, children's birthday parties, airplanes, boats, doctor's waiting rooms, and beaches. It's the buyer's call and we go where they want us.

12. **And here's the pitch:**

Break out your stats. Have a rough plan to find the house of their dreams with multiple options. Be present. Be professional. Be prepared. Be realistic. Get pumped, get them pumped, and you get the gig.

Most realtors these days don't officially open a buyer by signing an agreement. You need to show them houses immediately. Get in their face. Stay in their face. The more options, the better. Don't stop coming at them until they need a break or they fall in love. That's it. Nothing binds them to you except your performance, so you need to kill it. Options. Options. Options. Get creative. Know your hood. Know the next hood over. Assess value to ideas such as new construction, converted loft space, ocean front bluffs they never considered. Engage with maximum energy. Break out all the stops. Get them pumped!

I love repping the buyer. Before the meeting, research as much as possible based on them. Know their money. Know their hobbies. Know their Instagram photos, what they like, what they don't, what they want, and what they never thought possible. Your job is to sell them a new life. Do it. Sell. Close. They'll call you for this life and the next one when they're ready.

Chapter 15

OFF TO WORK: TAKE A BREATH FIRST

Whether your clients are buyers or sellers, there's a house for everybody and you're going to find it for them. You show up and show up on time, prepared. You fight for your client, 24/7, no matter what. You have the Game-Time mentality. You know the players. You know the field. You know the shot clock. You know the score. You and your Dream Team are dressed to impress and ready to make money. You know the rules of the game with your eyes on the prize.

It's all open, and you know how to find it. You know your hood. You know more than your 'hood. You know when and where to find your clients and where their new lives will begin. You know to ask. You know to listen. You know to market. You know your brand. You know your city. You're "Hollywood" in the Altman sense. You please people. You build communities. You serve. You're your own coach. You make money. Now, go to work.

Okay, the day has started. The phone is ringing. Emails are coming in. Every step along your way, this is "the work." You are not on TV.

Little negotiation follows little negotiation after . . . some more negotiation. You have listing appointments to schedule. Not all can accommodate. Make a deal. You have buyers to find homes for. Who? Where? When? Not all can accommodate. Negotiate. Make a deal. You're researching the MLS, contacting fellow agents and alliances for off-market properties in search of the perfect home to meet your clients' needs. You're not even out of the gym yet.

You're a genius who knows your new upcoming open house needs to feel alive and fun, so you're on the phone with a DJ. He wants too much money. Negotiate. Make a deal. You book him for a five-event package at a 30% discount. You're keeping expenses low and revenue high. Another email comes in, another phone call.

Wait, which property is this for? Take a breath. Your assistant yells out, "The lawyer's here for the Beachwood Canyon close." He's early. You haven't hung up with your new buyer, scheduling, scheduling, scheduling. This time or that? Which home first? He said a country kitchen. That's the right house, isn't it? You need to call the listing agent. Is this place accessible? Is the electricity even on? Lunch, if you get it, is hours away.

Here's a trick of the trade that sounds easier than it actually is – CHILL OUT! Once you find your flow, you'll get it. Take baby steps and it will all line up: one foot in front of the other. Break each task down into smaller tasks, and then plug away at them, one at a time. Make a list. Check it off. Next. Check it off. Next. Repeat.

You need to keep your head. If not, it shows. A flustered agent creates a flustered client. This does not build trust and confidence. This is not "Hollywood." Being "Hollywood" means that even when you're sweating through your suit, sprinting to your car, you have a carefree smile, because it's good, all good – all the time. Why? You're the agent who has it covered. You're not overwhelmed even when you are.

So, back to work, for real. This is still not TV.

Part II

THE WORK

Chapter 16

WORKING WITH BUYERS: PART CHEMISTRY, PART THERAPY

Before you dig into work, you'll want to dig deeper into agent/client relationships you've entered. You may be all over it when it comes to self-care on the job, doing what you do to stay chill under pressure. But your clients need constant reassurance that you are the one agent for the job. They need support.

We'll get to the nuances of the agent/seller relationship in the next chapter. For now I'm going to focus on buyers. But still, the first section about personality types applies to all clients. Remember: today's buyer may be tomorrow's seller.

So, in one way it's like your clients are your family. And you are like theirs. For this agent/client thing to work – to become a functional working relationship – you can learn to play off one another's styles, feelings, and emotions to the advantage you both. Win-win. This process may begin at an office meeting, a lunch, or at a first showing. It will continue to the close and often beyond. It's business but it's more.

In another sense, quality real estate agents are as much therapists as they are concierges, middlemen, facilitators of property – and family. But wait, the client is coach! You've got to sort this out. Read on.

ASSESSING PERSONALITY TYPES

How well do you really know your client? Sit down with their portfolio, you know, the one you've already constructed from everything you know about them. If you have partners in your firm, it's a team meeting. Who is this client? What do they want? What are they like?

Before you agree (or adapt your style) to work with this person, check with your co-workers and see which of you, personality-wise, is best suited to build this relationship. This goes back to the psychology of "mirroring" – knowing how to approach someone physically, in speech, grammar, and attitude. You must establish trust, confidence, and comfort as you establish business chemistry.

Know what to expect – craziness. You're going to get easy clients and you're going to get difficult clients. You're going to have the nightmare client who is all over the place, the client who can't keep a schedule, the client who won't let you breathe, constantly calling for an update. You'll have the clients who annoy you to death, trying to do your job for your then calling you about it.

You'll get the slow client, the stoned client, the abusive client, the client who twists your words so much you'll have to send a follow-up email right after every conversation to document your verbal exchange. (You should do this always, by the way.) This will get tough. Hang in there.

Take a breath. Your client is coach, the boss. You don't have to agree with their management style, but you have a goal. You promised to please, and in doing so you will make money. Baby steps.

With that said, you don't need to take crap all the time. Early in the Altman Brothers career, Matt had a client who turned from annoying to abusive. Matt hung in there, deal after deal, taking the hits for the team. Why? We needed money. We were growing a business. Eventually after half a dozen deals and three years, Matt had to break it off. The guy was a total jackass, constant drama and mean about it, too. He viewed Matt as the hired help, not a superstar on his team. Matt had enough.

We decided, Matt decided, that it wasn't worth his time or mental state to work with this "gentleman" anymore. So, he didn't. I recall his relief, the weight off his shoulders. I was relieved. This man would get Matt so pissed off that this negative energy became contagious.

As for me, I had a client who around the office we called "the slug." This guy always wanted me to show him houses, but he'd never buy. He'd fly in every few weeks and take a few weeks of my time with endless showings, never wanting to pull the trigger. Nothing was ever right for him. Nothing was good enough.

At first, I hung in there for the deal, the close. Then, I hung in there for the challenge, the perseverance, just to prove it to myself. I remember questioning in my head if this guy just wanted to be friends or if he was trying to pick me up. Still, I hung in a bit longer, my eye on the prize. This is the game, to hang in there, don't quit, and make the money.

After three years, I saw our longest running non-buyer client, just as I was about to waver and move on, at a party. "The slug" introduced me to a friend of his. "This is my agent," he said, "this guy's gold." The friend hired me right there. "The slug" solidified my open. I sold the new client a $13 million listing in our second month. That's why you stick around. That's why you put up with the nonsense. That's why we make money. And that is why you will, too.

ANALYZING THE BUYER

Beyond an initial meet, some research on Google, some questions asked and answered, and a study of their social media profiles, what is it you think you know about your buyer?

I may know their money and enough about their needs to know (or trust my gut) what kind of property to show them first. But that doesn't always mean THEY know their needs or what they think their needs are. Sometimes our lives change before our heads catch up. The best agents get to know the mind of the individual, what makes them tick.

If I have a new buyer, I'll set-up 10 homes to show based on the buyer's likes and dislikes. That requires 20 more little negotiations: I must coordinate a workable time with the listing agent as well as the buyer. Of those 10, I'll target the obvious requests first and throw in a few wildcards later, a few dreams – the first wave.

I watch my client. He keeps saying he loves modern as he drools over Mediterranean. I make a mental note. I know a little more of where to steer this guy. At the next few listings, I dig a little deeper, learn a bit more.

I had one client who kept telling me she wanted a four-bedroom house for now. She kept saying that. A four-bedroom house "for now." I couldn't help but think, "What was later?" Could I find her a four-bedroom now, then down the line get her a bigger home, having her and her husband as repeat clients? Maybe.

Then my wheels kept turning. Where was her husband? He's at work. She's driving this bus, and it's heading toward her wants, her needs. It seems they probably agreed on a reasonable mid-size house for their family now so as not to risk too much of their wealth.

Understandable, but I saw the signs. She was not pleased with the four-bedrooms I kept bringing her to. Did she really want that, or was she feeling confined by the agreement made with her husband? Maybe both if there were no reasonably priced five-or-more bedroom homes out there. I found one, a five-bedroom. I sent her a note, "This is your new home." She wanted to see it immediately.

Yes, it was more expensive, but not by much. We walked through. She fell in love. Immediately she asked me how was she going to sell it to her husband. I carefully considered the question, not to disrespect either one. "Spend a little more now, no need for transition later, you've already arrived, so no need to upgrade down the line. That nuisance could be avoided now with a little more investment." That was it. It was all she needed to hear, and the home was what she always wanted. The couple walked the house that night. She loved it, so he loved it. Even more, the rationale made sense to him and the price jump wasn't ridiculous. They made an offer the next day. Done. I closed.

If I hadn't been listening, if I had taken her word for it about a four-bedroom, I'd still be taking her around town, spending my time not pleasing her while I could have been pleasing another client. I could have been closing another property, making more money. She, my client, was just not ready to listen to herself. I helped her mentally get there, and I like to think her family is happier as a result. In fact, I know they are. They keep sending me business and they love their home. I had "learned" the buyer. Hell, I analyzed that buyer. I was agent as therapist. I worked and I closed.

CALMING THE BUYER'S FEARS

In the office we say, "Buyers are liars." They're not liars on purpose, unless they misrepresent funds, which I saw a lot in my days as a mortgage broker. Rather it's just that you haven't taught them who they are now and what they really like, or how to speak knowledgably about what it is they think they like, or how to minimize their real estate fears – all in the name of realizing the house of their dreams.

This is a good time to remember, from early in Part I, Daniel Kahneman's two systems of thinking. System 1 thinking is fast and intuitive. For a client buying a house, this simply means liking the aesthetic, the location, and the home itself based on its initial appearance. System 2 thinking is when a person digs deeper to analyze if that home will be the right fit for them in every other way.

Kahneman writes that there's a crossover between the two systems: System 1 thinking can be useful, and the so-called logical analysis of System 2 can result in a poor decision. As a solid real estate agent, you need to be aware and prepared that you'll have to help your client make a decision based on both types of thinking.

Sit the buyer down. Make a list of all of your showings. Detail the positives and the negatives. What did they react well to? What not? What did they say they wanted versus what they truly enjoyed? Price, materials, rooms, designs?

Be like Benjamin Franklin, who took the "Pro and Con" chart to a new level by assigning priorities to certain aspects, and help your buyer make such a list. The trends will appear. Properly assess the homes, the priorities, what was important, and what wasn't. Show them, analyze, discuss, and redirect your search accordingly. You now have a *map*. You now have mentally supported your client, and you have focused their priorities using a visual learning tool. They now view you as caring, attentive, and smart. They are comfortable. They are happy.

If your client is still a ball of stress, call in reinforcements. People freak out about uncertainty, complexity, and risk. People get overwhelmed with options, possibility, and expectation. Have you ever planned a wedding? Right. Me too. You may have watched it on BRAVO.

Your job is to minimize these fears, feelings, and emotions by going over every one of these aspects with your client. Put them at ease by acknowledging any concerns they have, from a kitchen gutting to a foreclosure.

If symptoms still persist, remember the goal and remember your own support systems. Your job is to get to the prize as fast as possible for all. Your job is to open, work, close. Call upon your Dream Team to consult on solutions to overcome the fears your client has. Life is not so scary when you see that the answers are attainable.

Call upon other agents. If I'm struggling to find a home in a super-aggressive market, then my client is struggling to. Bring in another agent, double your team, double your strategy, double your effort. You are agent as therapist. Put the buyer at ease. They'll take the ride longer. They'll hang in with you. You'll find what they want. You'll win. You'll make money.

Chapter 17

STRATEGIZING WITH SELLERS: GETTING READY FOR WAR

Selling real estate is like a game. The game is strategy. Drawing up the right plays and knowing when and how to implement them. The game is execution. Making it happen, embracing obstacles, getting creative, closing deals. The game is war.

THE BATTLE PLAN

You've signed a listing agreement. The gauntlet has been thrown. Your number one priority is to get the strategy worked out, the battle plan, the soldiers in place, then begin execution as soon as possible before the enemy can strike. In this case, the enemy is time. The longer the property is on the market, the more it will cower, weaken, die and rot. Come on, General. Don't lose your land, your power, your deal.

In a recent study, the median number of days on the market (DOM) in the United States was somewhere in the range of 65 to 70. Any number beyond that might reek of desperation to buyers who will low-ball the property, which will make the sellers take it off the market and relist it. A savvy agent or buyer can track the number of times a property has been listed on the MLS, but probably won't.

You've also signed an agreement that typically covers a three-to-six-month period. The DOM is always an issue in real estate. If you lose the first month to work issues – opening and closing the little deals to list, stage, show – and you don't watch the shot clock carefully on your listings, time's up, another enemy surfaces: fellow agents. They will take your land from you. They will conquer your listing. I would. Remember, all is fair in real estate and war.

The second rule of battle engagement in repping a listing is to never give up your intel. Never let the enemies know your moves, your strategy, or your secrets. When you sell a house for a client, no one should know why the client is selling. That's leverage that can be turned on you in a negotiation. Divorce, illness, and new job all scream a need to sell a house quickly and your opponent should – and will – use it against you. No matter the subject or location of the meeting, put on your poker face. If it's a call, keep emotion out of your voice. Be professional. Be straightforward. Be a soldier. Be a general. Be a closer.

A high-ranking real estate agent can focus on your tone and work it, searching for weaknesses. It's an interrogation. Always. You're fighting for land with an opposing side.

Usually, if your market is like mine, you're doing battle with the same 15 agents most of the time. You wouldn't give them surface-to-air missiles, so why would you tell them your client is fleeing an ugly divorce and has to be out in month? You wouldn't. You don't. Never. Real estate is obviously nothing like true war, but the analogy works. Run with it. In our world, this is battle.

Like war, a new listing requires strategy. How are you going to sell this house before the enemy forces come? Before the clock takes hold? Any secret weapons? Who can you call to maneuver in place the quickest possible deal? How can you create buzz? Who are your alliances? Who are your clients, willing and ready to buy?

Because of our high-end market and our high-powered or celebrity clients, we create mystique and desire through limited and targeted publicity. We often list the house off-market, not putting it on the MLS but on the local data feed for the west side of Los Angeles. Exclusivity is gold here.

People want what others can't have and our clients insist on it. No one wants to fight over land unless necessary. Our clients want to take what they can before anyone else, no hassle and all privacy. Otherwise, we'll go wide when need be. Specified guest list or not, our marketing strategy usually includes staging, still photography, drone video, advertisements, and open houses. We make a plan and we execute, marching forward, step by step at rapid speed. We build from there if needed, our lips sealed on the intent of our seller.

When you get a listing, you must develop your strategy. Watch the clock and strike quick. Don't get caught blindsided and you won't get surrounded. Be prepared at all times, always on the offensive, making moves. Ready the troops. Go to work. Go to battle. Go to war.

MANAGING THE TROOPS

But wait: In this case a large number of your troops are sellers, so this part of the battle plan requires some strategic commanding – call it managing and negotiating. It never ends throughout the arc of the close, but there are particular stressors when strangers start entering a house.

People get touchy about their homes. We all do. People see their houses as extensions of themselves. It's up to you to negotiate with your client. Remind them that this is their big launch, and first impressions matter when selling their house. Be up front and be clear about your expectations and what you need to do to make them money.

If the client is living on the premises, you'll need to begin negotiating about cleaning, staging, and photography, and get their agreement to leave the home during showings. Respect the owner, but in plain, get them the hell out of there! Send them to dinner, an NFL game, whatever. The owners, the entire family, and their pets must be out when you bring in possible buyers.*

It doesn't end there. Small repairs must be made. A running toilet can kill a showing in a second, whether you're showing a mansion or a double wide. If paint needs refreshing, get it done. The front walk could use some landscaping? Get it done. If the client isn't going to make these

---

* Side Note: When showing a buyer or another agent your client's home, always go outside to have serious conversations about the house. Sellers place cameras all around out of curiosity – and to monitor the agent. Don't get caught saying something that, while true, could come off as offensive to your client.

investments, and the house isn't at the price level to warrant staging out of marketing dollars, you've got to start negotiating.

I recently had to have the "update" talk with a repeat client. I sold them a modern house, state-of-the-art tech and design by the hottest builder/ architect duo in town – 10 years ago. "Stale modern" is a hard sell and this one had aged especially poorly. During the time the clients owned the house they hadn't made any updates. You have to discuss the impact on list price and expectations. This house may take a bit longer to sell, even in a strong seller's market.

With another property in the Hollywood Hills, I'm the third agent on a listing and the seller is just really fatigued. He asked me what the house needed – after all the fixes, he could not imagine what was keeping the house from moving. Of course it was overpriced – by about $6 million. The property's design was beautiful, but you could see right into it from the street and from the neighbor's houses. Privacy was an issue.

After much back-and-forth, during which I was both delicate and respectfully firm in reminding him that it takes money to make money, I finally got him to drop to a more realistic $29 million and he's investing $200,000 to privatize the house. Give to get. He worked with a landscape architect and planted trees between himself and all the surrounding houses. He installed tints in the windows and cool drop-down shutters. Now he has the right price and no one can stare inside. The house will sell.

You can't actually make people listen but you can insist and cover your ass. If clients really hear you, they may act. If not, document the warning and warn them again. Then remind them. After four potential buyers hate the front and won't go in, bring the client actual data on how the issues are impacting the work of selling the house. "Of the 27 people who have walked in, 19 have said the same thing." The more they hear, the more you might move them to action.

Also, notes are essential in managing clients. They like to ignore how others felt about a house or a feature so I remind them. Then, I will monitor these points as showings continue. Managing clients are a huge part of real estate.

Chapter 18

WEAPONS: LISTING LANGUAGE, INTERIOR DESIGN, AND STAGING

Boom, another listing! Return to the office with your new property to sell; hang it around your neck like a gold rope chain! Now, you need to capture a buyer. Whether you're listing the property on the MLS or it's off-market, get that first weapon in place. In this chapter we'll see what happens when we combine these weapons with others in our arsenal.

A KILLER DESCRIPTION

Arm the listed property with a killer description. Those buzzwords make this property appeal to any buyer, yet they are crafted to target an audience you know the home will speak to. This is "listing language."

You have to take on a few roles here: you're part journalist to report on the actual facts of the property, part salesman to hook the buyer, and – dare I say it – part poet (or lyricist). I'm not saying you need to be Maya Angelou or Bob Dylan, but . . . well, it would help. To be honest, I think the words of living rap legend Jay-Z embody what we agents do best: "I sell ice in the winter, I sell fire in hell, I'm a hustler, baby, I'll sell water to a well."

The Altman Brothers have someone in the office dedicated to writing listings. If you don't, I recommend enticing potential buyers with a little word-flow of your own by . . . uh, okay, borrowing it. Check the magazines, architectural descriptions, and other real-estate listings. Learn how the pros describe homes. Focus on the feature elements that attract.

Play it up, but not too much. Don't be stiff and boring, but don't over-do it with flowery language. It'll sound corny.

Beyond reporting that the house has five bedrooms and six baths, open with a list of desired amenities like a chef's eat-in kitchen, a three-car garage, and a state-of-the-art security system.

Then insert the "poetry" that will allow buyers to visualize what a life lived there might look like: "This house has floor-to-ceiling glass doors opening onto the infinity pool with views across the city, a classic example of the highly prized indoor-outdoor living of Southern California." Show, don't tell. Make the buyer feel like they're in the picture.

The Altman Brothers recently won a listing in the Hollywood Hills for an unbelievable estate. You'd think you were on an oil tycoon's ranch in Montana. We needed to describe the main house, Moroccan-style guest-house, and the grounds and stables with words that would jump off the page and kiss you. It ended up a little something like this:

"*Listed for $68 million: Once you pass through massive red gates, the owner has created 14-acres of pure tranquil magic, all in the preserved heart of Los Angeles.*"

Our listing language presented "*the quiet gardens that wind through the estate's buildings, creating a luscious island of peace inside the bustling LA metropolis. This is the house for a buyer who is beyond helicoptering to their country home. This house is for the buyer so successful they bring the country compound inside the city.*" I don't know about you, but I can feel the eyes of superstar Nashville country stars just lighting up.

Our words, carefully chosen, and the images we post, also carefully chosen, speak to certain clients we know will like the style of the house and grounds. Listing language matters. Language matters, period. Yes, you sink a lot of resources into photography and the internet, but your words must work too as an open. Your passion for homes and instincts about why a house is baller – without using the word "baller" – should be reflected in the listing language. Or, hell, maybe "baller" works depending upon the clients you're targeting. It attracts me. I'm baller.

Verbal thinkers respond with an "I hear you" and visual thinkers "see what you mean." Capture both types and you will attract buyers. Get the most cutting-edge images of the property you can and open hard in your listing language. Tailor it to the property, refine as you go, proofread everything, and above all, don't use brand names. You will get sued. That said, listing language is a huge weapon. It works. Your words will lead to showings and showings lead to sales. Close 'em.

KILLER DESIGN

Interior design is hot right now. It's on fire. With popular TV shows and magazines devoted to selling homes, the interior design industry has blown up! Americans are smarter than ever about how to create the world they want, whether it it's layered, moody, aspirational, clean, or reimagined. These are interior design words. Learn them. Know them. Use them, for real.

We've never had more slick, artistic buyers and sellers than right now. Classic to retro, natural to cutting-edge modern, Interior design sells. Interior design is art, and this art is killing it.

From 2018 to 2022, interior design industry projections jump from just over $2 billion a year to almost $4 billion, with the major centers being the two coasts, and states such as Texas, Illinois, and Colorado coming in a spicy third. Realtors should know interior design and, more importantly, interior designers working in their market.

Most towns have "celebrity" designers. Find them. Meet them. See their work. Not only are they a great source for insider referrals, as you are for them, but they also make you smarter about home design trends that you need to know as you show your listings. Keep an eye on interior trends. Read the magazines. Watch the TV programs. Learn the language. Take a class. Study. Research.

Know the "wish" list of your client and the public. Their money is your money. Their investment is your investment. If you're on your game with interior design, you can make the suggestions you need to stage a house properly (more on that to come), please your client, and close a deal.

This trend is so crazy now. It's a way of life. People engage with the process intensely; they consume media about house design so obsessively that it can drive you nuts.

Do you know the difference between Brazilian cherry and an ebonized hardwood? Get on it! Understand how to make lighting, an underutilized but critical aspect of interior design, change the dynamic of a space. Learn about floating vanities, quartz countertops, and large format tiles in the bathroom.

Closing big number deals is really my thing, but I could talk all day about the small details of design that make a house great. It's my business. It's yours, too. Kill it. Close. Make money.

STAGING FOR BATTLE

Staging is short-term interior design. Like an artist or architect, stagers play on emotions and the world around them to make a statement. Take a staged master suite, for instance, all cashmere throws and overstuffed pillows to counterbalance a bathroom with steam shower and Stone Forrest tub. The contrasting textures and luxurious amenities make a potential buyer want to call a loved one, break out some champagne, lay down, and end the search right there. A great stager gets this and plays into that vibe.

Staging creates a turnkey look that makes a buyer think of moving in on spot. More than once I've heard a buyer say jokingly "Forget the other showings. We'll take the furniture, too. We're staying!" Well, that's based more on wishful thinking than humor. In this town, turnkey is often a buyer's fantasy come to life. What's more convenient than stepping across a doorway and into a whole new life better than the one before? It's "Hollywood"!

Tons of data (realtor.com) tell us that staging brings up the price and perhaps more importantly moves the house off the market faster – 88% faster with a 20% increase in price, to be exact. Not only do I need to make the deal with the staging company, negotiating price and scheduling, the staging must be precise, on-point, to open the right buyer, in person and/or photographs.

In major markets, staging can run $15,000 to $100,000. This investment is no joke, but we're dealing with multimillion-dollar mansions here. Give to get. It's worth it. On the other hand, revitalizing an interior can be done creatively for far less "green" in a less high-powered market and still bring in high return. I'll get to that in a bit.

In LA, we typically spread the business among the two or three best staging companies in the industry. I often negotiate with the stagers, opening and closing small deals along the way for discounts on jobs. Offer credits in advertisements and signage at broker-only events. Help stagers get more business and they'll hook you up on pricing. I refer business to my stagers all the time and they to me.

Find a stager with the right chemistry for you as an agent and work with them with the close in mind. Stagers not only know the little details, such as the rule of odd numbers (cluster objects in threes), but they also look at the big picture, like the effects of color and light, and how the exterior and foyer have a huge impact on your ability to close a sale.

I've had buyers close to committing, but kind of on the fence, and I've gone back in with the stager before the second tour. In a Bel-Air listing we rearranged a media room for family play, complete with a Wii console and remotes, games downloaded and ready to play. The people went crazy for it. For one listing in Malibu, we lit lanterns all over the back deck, turned on the gas fire, set the table, arranged outdoor pillows and throws and left. We didn't stay but just left champagne on the table and let the buyers pretend it was home. We sold both houses.

That's what I mean about killer ideas. Through design, a stager puts an image into the buyer's head of how they want to live. And with the stager, we sell a dream the buyer never considered.

Even better, the stager assists the close by diverting the eye from the flaws of the house. The more imaginative, the better: To enhance a dark corner one stager I hired set-up a nineteenth-century Japanese screen, arranged a furniture grouping in front of it, and lit it from below, Boom! Buyers responded. The Altman Brothers closed!

Make sure your stager knows the science behind it all. How color in itself can raise the price of a house and speed up the close. In recent years, Zillow undertook a massive analysis of 32,000 photographs to see if color impacted the final sale. The test set controls for square footage, location, age of house, and date of transaction.

Need to amp up those areas for first impressions, the curb appeal? The front door, painted shades of navy blue, or a dark gray or charcoal, raised the final price by $1,514, on average. Exteriors painted "greige," a combination of gray and beige, sold for an average of $1,526 more. Yellow added about $1,300 to the value of kitchens. In 2018, yellow is out and blue is in, with the average price increase rising to $1,809. Oatmeal or taupe-colored living rooms added $1,800 and the new price-enhancing color for bedrooms is a calming cerulean or cadet blue, which adds $1,856 to the price.

It's crazy, right? Starting out in this business, I knew different colors were hot at different times in attracting up-to-date buyers, but upping prices like that? It caught me off-guard. But if you're anything like me – "Hollywood," and by this chapter you should be – then your heart rate must be pumping at these price increases, and you'll start to study up like I did. Just know, the colors that fatten your pocket change by the season, year to year, so stay on your staging game.

This Zillow data is proof of the power of staging. If you want to make money, this data matters. So if you have a listing that's struggling, paint the damn door! What's a can of paint? Designer brands can be had for less than $30 a gallon. You don't want to do it? Call your Dream Team or your assistant. Any fool can put up self-adhesive kitchen backsplash tiles. Big-box home stores sell them for under $50. Work with a stager to introduce the blues into the house and reshoot the photographs. Retile a backsplash with up-to-date color. Make the upgrades that attract. Keep up with trends.

So find your favorite stager. Get them on your team. Open and close a deal with them. Negotiate. Offer a lower price if they'll do your next three houses. Get what you need out of it. And what is that? A sale. A deal. A close. More money for your client. More money for you.

Make stagers part of your Dream Team. You'll kill it, especially in the high-end market. You'll see the spike in the buyers' eyes as well as in their offers. Someone will bite and you'll close.

I have stagers completely immersed in the visual language of international and modern as well as stagers gifted at more traditional, Tudor and Craftsman-style homes.

Just make sure the staging you do for your photos or video stays in place for your real-life showing, or your client will call you out. An agent will call you out. Hell, one agent I know undid the staging but left the videos online. I snagged the listing. He should have read this book.

Chapter 19

THE KILLER COMBO: DRONE AND 360° PHOTOS PLUS STAGING

I introduced you in Part I to branding weapons we use – cutting-edge technology such as drones and 360-degree cameras – to shoot our listing promos. Let's put those together with still photography and staging to get the most of creating real-Hollywood-world virtual reality. This is Hollywood, right? All three make a killer-combo strategy as we open, work, and close.

Let's start with photography and cinematography, media I've learned more about through real estate than by being on television. You don't need to be a complete expert in these fields, but you need to know someone who is, and you need to know what not to do. Although I don't hold the camera, I know how my listing should be shown on film and linked online; in other words, I know how to put it in your face.

Who sells houses? Well, we sell houses. What helps us sell houses? That's right, the top-notch photos and videos we post online. This heavily involves staging, but we'll get there in a second. Point is, if you think great houses sell houses on their own, you can think again. Focus: lights, camera, action.

In 2015, 100% of all homebuyers accessed the internet in their search; 86% watched video of their new community; and 70% toured the insides of properties online. That data is why we invest in the highest level of interior and drone photography our market has to offer. That's how effectively these images sell houses.

It makes me cringe, but we've all seen it, an agent in the middle of the street waving a smart phone, attempting to grab a few non-blurry shots of a listing. What are you kidding me? That won't do it. Don't even try.

With 95% of all buyers using the internet to search for homes (National Association of Realtors, 2017), you have to look sharp, a real player. Not like some high school kid in film class. You're "Hollywood." A baller. In your world iPhones are for ballers who communicate with sellers and buyers to make money. Real money. Altman money. Not for making videos. When it comes to a photo, "sharp" is the word, literally. Cutting-edge technology says, "I'm ahead of the game, and you want to be where I am." Here are more stats from Redfin (2013): Professionally photographed homes in general sell for $3,400 to $11,200 more over list in the $200,000 to $1 million range. When Redfin analyzed the top 10% of its sharpest listing photos, the data showed they sold over list 44% of the time rather than the average 13% of amateur-shot, fuzzier photos. Sharp photography also affects the time a house sits on the market: In the $400,000 to $500,000 range, 64% of the professionally shot houses sold within six months, compared to 46% for homes photographed with a "point-and-shoot" smart phone. Are you with me? You're an adult, a businessperson. Act like it. Hire a professional.

Bring your stagers and photographer together to shoot the house in its best light. If the property is rural the photography should feel rural, breadbasket rural, bed & breakfast, Norman Rockwell, I love America, babbling brook *A River Runs Through It* rural. Have a peaceful, natural world vibe and show how the house integrates with its surroundings, from the outside in to the inside out. Shoot the living room to capture the picture window, the open field, the rolling hill, and the stone wall leading to the giant oak tree. Don't forget the hawk circling the sky beyond the sunflower patch. Rural.

As for suburban houses, they work best in bright daylight, accentuating blue skies and long green lawns. If the backyard is glorious, go to the highest spot in the house and have them shoot down on it or photograph at twilight. Show the scenes the potential buyer will see "forever" if they buy the house.

Part of your closing strategy is working with your "image" people to capture the house in the best way to sell it. If you've got a listing that is an entertainer's dream, it's common sense to stage a series of shots of the house at night, lit and ready to greet guests. If the house has an unreal pool and outdoor kitchen, set it up and shoot it. Take strengths and blow them up big. The things you know will sell the house should be front and center in photographs and listing language.

Take a good number of shots. I'd say get 20 to 30 crisp selling images of all areas of the house with special focus on the bathrooms, master suite, kitchen, and living area, all of which need glorious, hyper-clean, hyper-crisp shots. As you progress through the sale, you will need to rotate the photos as you get feedback and go through the price-drop phase. Think of the new content as a re-launch. Your photographer should prep and load your photos, editing out distortions and odd mirror reflections. The devil is the details here, and you the agent are God. So, if you love houses like I do, you love this part of the work.

Now, in major markets, professional still photography is the norm, but video interior tours and aerial drone footage is taking over, as you've seen on the Altman Brothers site (thealtmanbrothers.com). Video is on the rise. You get more clicks and views online with video, and there's a lot of technology available to track views and provide you with leads. Research it. Use it. You can follow up with additional house details using auto-mated emails, and even reach out directly if a particular lead catches your eye. Get with it.

We've been using aerial drone video to sell our listings for a long time now and all the Altman houses get this treatment. Don't forget, video pulls up your Google rankings. Make sure your listing videos are attached to your website. We post ours on Vimeo and attach it to the Altman Brothers site. Bar code technologies allow potential clients to access the exact house video and details of a particular house on smartphone with no scrolling.

Now, my clients stage because the property values are so high, and our marketing budget mirrors that. But we all know that's relative. A $150,000 home can be just as essential to the wealth of another client, yet that client can't justify covering the staging cost. If that's the case, you need to convince them to up their game to help move the house in that critical first 30 days. Negotiate staging, even offer to split it with the owner from your commission.

In many markets, staging doesn't require mad cash like LA or New York. Push it as far as you can, negotiating all angles. Does the client have an interior designer friend? If you hired someone to offer advice, would they update? If the answer is still no, you need to decide if it makes sense financially for you to stage. Most likely, it does. Give to get. Be a shark. Matt would say, "think bigger" and I agree with him. You're building a business here.

Walk the owners through their own house. Point out all the personal photos and objects that need to be put away. Help them roll up carpets and expose wood. Open the drapes or remove them completely and let natural light flood in through clean windows. Any kind of darkness inside the house is a no-go. What are they hiding? Get it lit. Mirrors add brightness and pillows and fabrics add color, both a small investment. Don't be cheap. Again, this is your business, your life. Make money and enjoy it.

Now, a good rule for bedrooms and bathrooms is to go for the "luxury hotel" look. Use white fluffy towels in the bathroom; stash personal objects out of sight. A beautifully made bed with a textured throw spread across it completes the luxury look you want in the most intimate spaces. Any one of the discount home stores (brick-and-mortar and online) or big box retailers will have a wide variety of decorative pillows, towels, and bed linens. Mirrors make a room appear larger and are right on trend; replace any less-than-compelling art with mirrors and bring even more light in.

If rooms are cluttered, move larger pieces out to make it feel larger. Ask the seller to group furniture into smaller conversational units known as "vignettes" in interior design; create a sense of life. Set the table and freshen up place. Make it smell good. Spritz scented spray into the air, or use reed diffusers with essential oils – citrus, lavender, sandalwood, floral. A deep clean by professionals is certainly not going to break the bank, nor is a can of paint to fix up an interior wall.

Don't forget curb appeal. Even in the most expensive cities in America, a flat of flowers is still under $25 and the homeowner should plant and put out the welcome mat.

Think you're done? Nope. The cameras are gone, but the staging stays. Invite the buyers. You already prettied it up. Now show it. You made the listing gold for the cameras, now show it off in the flesh. Have an open house the way you shot it. It's a party – food, drinks, music, furniture, and a new home. I'll meet you there.

But wait. The store wants their furniture back before open house day? Negotiate, which you should have already done. Make a deal. Extend it. Give to get. Approach a furniture store about providing some show-stopping pieces for you to hang on to throughout the selling process. Why doesn't the store start a home-staging business as a part of its marketing efforts?

Have signage to give credit to the store lending the furniture. Or have one of their representatives – most have an in-store interior designer – work the open house, handing out information to all. Hell, let them sell the pieces right off the floor of the open house if you want. It works and the furniture sale advertising will bring in even more potential clients for you to open. Negotiate. Make a deal.

Remember, there is nothing in real estate that cannot be negotiated. There are no rules, just the limitations of your own time and energy as you open, work and close. And if you think open houses don't matter anymore just because you shot a high-tech video, you don't know much about selling real estate. Are you "Hollywood" or not? Let's keep working.

Chapter 20

ON THE BATTLEFIELD: MORE ON OPEN HOUSES AND BROKER'S OPENS

I'm not trying to be cocky here; it's kind of just fact. I am the open house king. I might even lobby to trademark the term. Open houses are like birthday parties to me, except year after year they make me feel younger, more alive, ready to open, work, close. I love 'em. Not only do I work the listing the open house is for, but also I meet new people, form alliances with new brokers and industry players, and open new clients.

I'm having a hard time talking about war and battle here because an open house just puts a smile on my face. Then again, so does the fight of the deal, the battle of real estate, the war of negotiation. Have I mentioned that I love those too?

Open houses are the cornerstone of selling strategy. They mark the open battlefield and the beginning of the bloodshed. (I introduced open houses for brokers, insiders, and buyers in Part I and touched on the basics.) Now it's time to explain how you use them to plow your way through the front lines, taking names, weeding out the weak on your way to the king you plan to dethrone.

Always keep learning. Agents worth their salt will continue to check out other agent's open houses, even off the clock, if there is such a thing in this game. You'll see what works and what doesn't. Even today with a family of my own, I'll slip out on Sundays for a couple of hours to visit open houses in neighborhoods I'm curious about. I can get face-to-face with real buyers and keep my eye on the street.

Celebrity clients are great – as is their money – but I sometimes miss people that grind to pay the bills: people who don't have assistants and money managers; people who keep me in tune with the game at a down-to-earth level. It's like an NBA player going back for some street ball in the old hood. You remember the roots of the game. You take those roots and amp them up when you're back at work at a higher level. Never forget where you came from, or you'll risk losing the edge that got you there.

When it comes to the real estate open house, much of what we agents do has been done before. We're not reinventing the wheel here. We're just perfecting a new tire. That said, how is your wheel different? To be creative, to be fresh, it often helps to take a standard format and find your personal twist.

For instance, we at Altman Brothers hold open houses for buyers before we do broker's caravans. We've turned the norm on its head. Let me explain:

Open houses are part of the work of closing a sale, but they're also powerful active opens. Once the listing is back in the office and prepped to hit the MLS, we put the house on the market on Friday and show it to the public on Sunday. Then brokers see it on Tuesday, the exact opposite of how most realtors roll their listings out. Showing the public first accomplishes two main goals.

First, some house buyers come with their agents but many don't. We land new clients with the potential of double-ending the deal. They may not have an agent to list their house should they be interested in either the one we're showing or another listing we represent. That's the active open. If nothing works out on this house, we've still broadened our reach for potential new business.

Second, we want a buzz on the street before agents walk through. Few worlds are as gossipy as real estate. If home buyers all call their agents on Monday to report a cool new house that just hit the market the day before, the local real estate industry takes notice. Tuesday's broker's caravan takes on a buzz, and we've launched the listing with as much velocity as possible.

WHO TO INVITE?

Now, much like any industry, real estate is full of the usual suspects, the same top dogs. Some stats say that 20% of the registered agents sell 80% of the real estate, or the equally unbalanced 10% of the registered agents sell 90% of all the real estate. In my speeches, I use the number 5% and 95%. The numbers vary city to city, but let's just say that a very few people sell a whole bunch of real estate. In Los Angeles, I'd say the same 15 people sell just about everything.

That being said, it's not hard to come up with guest lists for your broker's caravans. Announce them via the important feeds in your market and then email invitations to the top 10% or 20%. Make sure you bump into these agents at your event.

Be on your game. I can walk through a house and assess it in a hundred seconds. Most agents can. They walk in, move through quickly, hang around to make some calls or send texts, and leave. That means you have just a few minutes of their attention to engage before they wander off.

That conversation has to be smart – you can't bullshit a bull-shitter, as a bull-shitter once said. Be focused. Get to the point. They know why they're there. You know why they're there. No need for much song and dance. So get in their face and get to business. You don't have to be crude about it, but say what you came to say and keep them on their toes. With me, they're expecting Josh Altman, maybe the same shark they think they see on television. I like to catch them a bit off guard. Put them to work.

When I approach an agent at a caravan for my listing, I try to flip the expectation of my attack into a question for them. Instead of running my pitch in selling my listing, I'll ask something like "What would you say about this house if you were me?" The agent relaxes into answer, often gives me great ideas for my pitch, and ends up thinking that showing the house to their client was their idea. You can turn a coalition of the unwilling into the willing with a few well-placed questions. Pluck their answers and insert them in your pitch. Pros help pros, even when they don't realize it.

While I like to take most of the credit for the Altman Brothers killing it as much as we are, it is our reach to so many others that has fueled our success. We can attribute that to open houses and broker's caravans. Say 50 agents pass through my listing. The law of averages says it will get a couple of mentions to a third party, perhaps even a buyer. Do the math. One person leads to 3, which leads to 10, and so on.

Network through a caravan, Everyone's just a few phone calls away. You can get to anyone in this day and age. Get creative. Be bold. Network. Make the call. Get in their face. Form a relationship. Give the invite. Get ready to make a friend, even if you hate them.

WORK THE PARTY

Everyone wants to be the cool kid who throws an awesome party. That's not your job. You are there to open, work, close. You are there to sell the house. Not to overshadow it. Not to trash it. Not to even enjoy it, though you'd better. You are there to sell it. Play to the house. Let the style of the home, neighborhood, and staging be the focus. Be subtle. Be clever. Be simple.

Food at LA broker's caravans is always over-the-top and usually pointless. A $36 million listing might get you made-to-order omelets and a salad bar. Some realtors love it. They'll brag about their events' spread. Some even go for the food. Me? I'd rather be showing a house, locking down a deal, or hanging out with my wife and daughter.

Costly catering can eat up marketing budgets and with the 5% / 95% split of agents doing the work versus those who don't, I don't see how feeding 95% of the people who don't sell houses will help sell a house. If you want to close, focus on other closers. Focus on the house. Maybe serve a few drinks to loosen them up.

We recently had a listing in the brokers' caravan for a penthouse in downtown L.A. The area was a dead part of the city for a while, but now has exploded with luxury real estate, and a lot of old movie theater marquees from the original LA Broadway exist now as storefronts, giving the area a very old New York vibe. The place we were showing had three glass walls with views towards Santa Monica. We had an elegant violinist and served martinis and canapés. It was swanky, elegant, old school, refined. The refreshments were inexpensive, right for the property, and crumb-less.

Just like an over-produced video, an over-produced buyers caravan can hijack the focus from the house. Find an appropriate entertaining idea for the property. I wouldn't serve those same martinis at an open house for a Spanish-style ranch in the Valley. I'd go with a single Spanish acoustic guitarist, Rioja wine, with charcuterie and cheese. Subtle. Simple. Clever. Don't overproduce it. It's just not worth it, and I'll tell you why.

We represented a fantastic house and wanted to give it a power-launch. Through connections, we partnered with Rolls-Royce for an event. They parked their newest cars in the driveway and underwrote the party. *Million Dollar Listing LA* covered the opening and the camera loved those cars, giving Rolls-Royce a good bang for their marketing buck.

What happened with the listing? Nothing. For real, nothing happened. Not one buyer or their agent came back because of that opening. I still have agents come to me all the time and say, "let's do an open with Rolls-Royce for my $2.9 million listing." My answer? "Hell no! The car is worth more than the house." That party was great reality television but bad business. We'll never do it again.

WHAT ABOUT NEIGHBOR(HOOD)S?

I've talked a lot about neighborhoods in the Part I, so by this point you've done the research, right, checked the biggest players in internet real estate listings – Zillow, Trulia, Redfin – and made a cheat sheet in case someone throws a question your way. Beyond selling the neighborhood, consider what other details will affect hosting an event that will bring a crowd. How's the parking? How's the street activity? Consider the neighbors. Nothing dampens an open house like the guy from across the street cursing you out in the driveway or the kids next door hitting a baseball through the window. Is the area safe? Is the street gated, restricting your guests? Is local law enforcement or security aware you'll be drawing a crowd?

After discussing all angles with your client, circle the block at the time you plan on hosting your open house before you even schedule the event. Look for any potential issues that could throw off your open house. You wouldn't believe how others may act when they feel annoyed or territorial when strangers invade the neighborhood. Get ahead of this by mere acknowledgement. Knock on the adjacent doors, introduce yourself, explain the scenario, and make sure all are at ease. You may even land a new client.

SELL STRONG POINTS AND KNOWLEDGE

Let me beat you over the head with this piece of advice of Part I: Sell, don't tour.

Anyone can point to a bathroom and say, "Here's the bathroom. Isn't it nice and big?" Come on. How about: "This bath has double sink vanities, state-of-the-art rainfall shower, granite tiles, tons of storage, and a soaker tub. You won't find a bathroom like this one for 30 blocks in every direction. It's killer. I wish I had a bathroom like this."

You have to sell, sell, sell. To do that, you have to love what you're selling. The passion needs to show on your face and in your voice. Believe it or they won't believe you. People need to get excited. You need to hook them. You need to wow them. You need to close. You can do this at an open house or later, at a private showing.

So many mediocre agents dismiss the importance of guiding the walk through, but it's as important as the house itself. If you don't accentuate the strengths of the homes you sell, and paint the picture of what it's like to live in them, potential buyers may not see the vision on their own. If this is a weakness for you, then work on it until you get it right. Rehearse it. Create a script for yourself if you need to. Punch up the selling points. Punch up the passion. There's no other option. Adjust, adapt, and overcome. Open. Work. Close. Sell.

Get enthusiastic. If you can't legitimately find something special in the house that warrants getting excited, get creative. Stage it even. Almost every house, every room, has something to accentuate in sales. It's your job to find it and "frame it" for the consumer. It's a pitch, a nudge – a positive way to view the real estate, to sell. Make comparisons to other houses for sale in the neighborhood. You know buyers have probably walked through them if they're in the middle of a serious house hunt.

Focus on the house as a whole – the architecture, the design, and the history. These details are important to people, as if by knowing a home's history they will own a piece of that too. Use this. You need to be able to talk knowledgably about all styles of architecture in and out of the neighborhoods you are selling.

Most regions of the United States are characterized by particular styles, and when you sell houses, it's a great point of reference for you and your clients. Matt and I have made modern residential house design a specialty of ours because we love it, and modern is a major style on the West Coast.

The Stahl House, for instance, designed by the renowned architect Pierre Koenig, is an extraordinary midcentury modern built on a sliver of a Hollywood hill in 1959. All concrete and glass, it pulls views from the Griffin Observatory to the Pacific right into the living room. This house is a point of reference for any passionate modernist out here. After studying this iconic structure, we actually got the chance to sell Koenig's personal home – and we did so for a profit.

Every state has famous houses and architects, and the more you understand the culture behind the design, the more you inform them, the more you impress them, and sell.

Try drawing a comparison between your listing and a famous architectural design. For example, if you live in New England and are the listing agent for a spectacular modern home rising over the potato fields of Connecticut, you might want to invoke Phillip Johnson's Glass House in New Canaan.

If you are in the Midwest, the Prairie-style as defined by Frank Lloyd Wright is a good touchstone. Dallas can't get enough "Tuscan." Colonials are beloved all over the country. While one may claim that one-story homes speak to the huge number of baby boomers hitting retirement, if you're in Arizona, the single story is "cool" due to a hot climate that requires low-cost air-conditioning.

Your business is houses. Be an expert on houses. People trust experts. Do you spend millions of dollars with amateurs or with experts?

Chapter 21

PRICE DROPS ARE NOT ALWAYS DOWNERS

You know how this goes to start. Sellers are often unrealistic about the price of their home. And we get it. They want to make money, not lose it. But markets change. They fluctuate. Homes depreciate from what they once cost or what someone first paid.

I already prepared you during Part I to arrive at an initial listing price. Now we need to discuss the continued price drops you may have to face with your client throughout the selling process. Remember, a price drop doesn't have to be a downer. It could be the strategic momentum needed to close – a positive rather than a negative move.

Sellers, as we know, often insist on overpricing. They want a larger return and they usually have deep attachments to a house. So we developed a "script" you can use to navigate the price-lowering negotiations with sellers during the work phase. Letting go of a fantasy price is tough, but the looming threat of double mortgages can make a client jump off the roof. Seriously.

Part of your job is to be reality checker who reminds sellers that the house will sell when it is priced right for the market. Again, Redfin says houses in the United States are for sale an average of 70 days, and realtor. com put the number at 65. In some of my territory, if a house gets listed at all it's considered a loser. You're always on the shot clock. You have to move fast. You have to sell. You have to close. Or the property dies and rots on the battlefield.

Not only does your client and the house need to be in line with the market but also, if you overprice you'll knock out potential buyers who won't even take a look. You'll have to go hunting for them hard when the listing price is lowered. All of that adds time to your days on market. This gives the vibe that something is wrong with the house.

On the flipside, if you price too low you'll be flooded with offers, and then you'll do a lot of sifting and analysis. Even worse, you might not get the best price for your client. The goal is to set the price correctly with (and for) your client from the door. But again, that's easier said than done considering emotional and financial demands. Any number of things can keep a house from moving as planned. If you can't identify them, you're only choice is to drop the price.

Matt and I aren't working pocket-listing Hollywood legend compounds every day. Our bread and butter houses, owned by the clients who keep our business thriving, are in the $2 to $4 million range. Their homes account for a large part of their personal wealth. We begin setting sellers up for the "price drop convo" as soon as we begin work. It's part of the strategy and should be mentioned during every telecom, report, and meeting, along with news about the pricing of comps.

Your market might allow you many more weeks on sale before you feel you need to renew strategy. In ours, we have to turn on a dime. So, we make sure to document every interaction with a potential buyer or another agent and we bring this seller the news. We let the market speak for itself through these interactions. You are a reporter here, not a critic.

Then, you need to take control. You need to be aggressive. In this case, you need to find a middle ground with your client, the one you've been seeding. You need to drop to the right price that will get this house sold before it freezes altogether.

Price reduction is so much easier if you've been communicating with your client and have established the "team" mentality. Don't call for the first time in weeks and hit them with a price drop. They'll feel blindsided and screwed over. It'll piss them off and maybe get you fired. Keep them involved and they'll see that a price drop is just part of the game. They won't be able to ignore it. They'll argue at first, but the facts are the facts.

Next, since you're a "Hollywood" agent you've been keeping records of every agent and potential buyer you've talked to. You know who liked the house, but not the price. You know the buyers you can go to, now that you've dropped to a certain number. Whenever you reduce, have this list ready. Pick from the top, and give someone an exclusive. They have to see it now or no chance.

If that doesn't work, go back to the list and go wide. Call all agents and let them know you're dropping the price. Use the drop as your fast break to move ahead, get more showings, and get offers. Post new visuals and redo the listing language. Attract a new wave of interest. Reduction is a trigger for action – a moment in the process for you to move the work phase forward. Refresh the presentation. Build the buzz. Play up the urgency. Let them know they must see the house now because it will not be around much longer at this new price.

We try and make whoever we call feel like we singled out them (and only them). So we say, "You've got to see this NOW. I can't hold it at this price. Get back here! I need to know if you're going to do this!" Price reduction is another use-it-or-lose-it moment. It's a reality for every real estate agent who has ever lived, so use it to your advantage.

Negotiating with the client is a huge part of this job, so here's a schedule for the price-drop conversations we all "love" so much:

1. Execute listing agreement
   a. Strategize and execute marketing plan
   b. Schedule and execute open house and brokers' caravan
   c. Document, organize, and strategize feedback
   d. Set up communication system with client

End of Week I
2. Client reporting
   a. Discuss potential buyers' feedback on house and price
   b. Update and manage expectations
   c. Discuss essential updates to the house based on open house feedback
   d. Tell the client about upcoming showings
   e. Schedule an update
   f. Refine list of potential buyers based on feedback

End of Week II

a. Document and report potential buyers' feedback
b. Tell the client about upcoming showings
c. Schedule an update
d. Refine list of potential buyers based on feedback

End of Week III

a. Document and report potential buyers' feedback
b. Begin price drop discussion based on market (potential buyers') feedback
c. Suggest new price (let them get used to the number)
d. Schedule an update
e. Refine list of potential buyers based on feedback
f. Prep new marketing materials for MLS and adverts

End of Week IV

a. Document and report potential buyers' feedback
b. Negotiate price drop
c. Present new marketing plan
d. Use feedback to recreate listing language and select new images
e. Communicate drop to interested buyers
f. Release new marketing materials to MLS and adverts
g. Return to Week I, repeat

Discuss any negative comments with the seller, especially recurring ones. Negative buyer feedback, motivation, and schedule are your golden hammers when negotiating price drops with your client. The date your seller wants to move out is a hammer. The fact they grow weary of the process of selling a property is a hammer. So is the "why." Information is always useful; never stop listening even when you don't like what you hear.

Use the comments of others to help shape your client's point of view. Reinforce the need for the right price to accomplish what the client wants of you: to sell the house. Price drops are a part of that. Help your seller make connections between the price and the negative comments; move them from System 1 to System 2 thinking, if you can. Show them the comps again and discuss the market. People aren't always rational when it's their home. Real estate agents are the reality check.

Repeat the price reduction schedule until you sell the house or the listing expires. Go in with a new plan — add an agent from another company with the right reach or create a more aggressive or completely different marketing campaign — and remind your client that when the price meets the market, it will sell and someone will love their house because there's a house for everybody, even my insane friend Rich.

I was selling a glass-walled house in the Hills built on a wide ledge of earth hanging off a hill. It had a perfectly configured infinity pool, outdoor seating, firepit, outdoor kitchen, and small perfectly square patch of grass. The place was sick, but funky. Every person I walked through liked it but wouldn't make an offer because of its pointed entryway. It did hit a sour note, design-wise, especially among the neighboring houses. I had to have the price-drop convo a few times on this one.

After the third price drop I was taking a hard-partying client higher up the hill to see another listing, and as I passed I said, "Look there, Rich. That's my listing, too. You sure could find that one coming home wasted." He laughed, said he wanted to see it real quick on the way to our other showing, and I walked him through. He made an offer that day and I double-ended it. As it turns out, there's even a perfect house for crazy Rich, but he would have never offered at the original price. No one would have. Again, it's all part of the game.

Chapter 22

GO WIN THE WAR

You've got five minutes before the client shows. Get in the zone. You're a warrior, guns blazing. You're about to take a potential buyer to see a dream home. They're not a potential buyer, they're your buyer. You love this house and you're going to make them love it too. This is the house of *their* dreams. Apologize for even standing in their living room. This is your buyer. The commission check is in your pocket. Get ready for that new car. You're about to earn it. You're "Hollywood." Open. Work. Close.

Here's the big picture: You've kept your head. One foot in front of the other as you've scheduled showings, meetings, open houses, all while juggling your listings, finessing other agents into getting a deal worked, a deal done. You've sized up your clients appropriately, meeting their needs, mirroring their lives only to show them the life they always dreamed of having.

Your working relationships are solid, your client chemistry gold. You've featured every property in the best possible way with stellar listing language and cutting-edge videos that frame the strengths of each and every room. Your staging game is killer, awesome, on-point. You'd live in each listing if you could – and you can, but you'd rather sell it. You'd rather make money, and you're pulling it in hand over fist. You're a soldier, a general, a tank. You've taken all of your clients through the process of selling and/or buying their home, mapping out their likes and dislikes, playing off their emotions to keep the eye on the prize, the close.

Each step of the way, you've held your clients' hand as if you were family. You are agent as therapist. You've gotten them over the hump. Open houses, you've nailed them. Broker's opens, you've worked them, networking, pleasing all. Listings, whether on the market or pocket, are your best friends. You're cool, comfortable, confident, a reach that knows no bounds.

Price-drops, you've used them as strategy. Alliances, they come to you, grateful. You've managed your sellers, launching their products and their homes – their lives rocketed into better ones because of you. They love you. You love you. I may even love you. Now, here comes another one. Here comes the job. Here comes the prize. You're "Hollywood"! It's time to for the final battle, the big bomb, the negotiation. It's time for the Altman Close.

Part III

THE CLOSE

Chapter 23

MAKING AN OFFER

You're at the table. You're ready for war. Let's do this. It's not rocket science. It's finesse. It's cunning. It's knowing when and how to play it.

Making a real estate offer by definition seems to be a simple thing. It's proving you can pay for a property, on a specified closing date. If repping a buyer, you inform the seller what the buyer wants to pay for the house, and you specify any other terms the buyer wants. If repping a seller, inform the buyer what the seller wants as well as any terms. Easy, right? Wrong. Pay attention.

The moment money appears, things get real and they get real fast. The pressure of the clock is on, down to its final seconds. You have to move; to be quick and precise the nearer you get to the close. Owners begin moving out in their head. Buyers want to get the most for their money, sometimes demanding ever-escalating concessions from the seller. People get weird.

Recently, we almost lost a $14 million sale because the air conditioning units were at life expectancy. The buyer wanted to call the deal off for a $3,500 dollar fix. We ran over there and hired someone to install a new air-conditioning unit with our own money. We handled it. We closed. If you're not ready, if you don't know your client, and opponent's head and heart, then you haven't paid attention and things will get rough. If you're armed with your weapons, ready to pull the trigger, then this part will be as fun for you as it is for me.

SETTLING ON THE PRICE

First, because of the laws governing real estate, you must do it by the book. Don't get sued. Don't break laws. Don't lose your license. Don't get locked up. A trail of paperwork comes in handy if anyone feels discriminated against or cheated later on. No matter whether you are buyer or seller, an offer isn't an offer until it's been submitted in writing. Track your paper and follow up. Don't be negligent. Cover your ass.

Now, in the state of California, real estate offers have a 72-hour expiration date. By law, if you've offered or received an offer, you have three days to accept or reject. In an extremely pressurized time frame, a killer real estate agent works hard during that 72 hours.

Prepping for the offer, you size up your opponent, not only the seller, but also the seller's agent. If you've been working the simple formula of open, work, and close in the many micro-deals that got you here, you're now on the mountain top where the big offers live. You're primed to attack.

If I'm the agent offering on a property, I cut the time by two-thirds and give the seller 24 hours to respond or I retract the offer. Collapse time to raise your leverage; you've now got the other agent moving faster to meet your deadline. I also collapse time because people lose interest quickly. A buyer may say, "I love this house!" on Tuesday and start second-guessing themselves by Wednesday.

Real estate time requires you move because pressures move in from all directions; you're now managing the seller's needs along with your buyer's. He or she now has a day to find the other offers if you're the first, and we all know the first is usually the best. If this agent is off their game in any way, they have no time to recreate what happened. That's why you must view everything you say and do, even the first conversation, as part of a close. That blink of an eye between offer and answer is huge opportunity for a really smart seller.

Call the other agent before you offer. Find out if other offers have come in. "Expecting any day now" is often the answer. That doesn't count. Offers in hand are what matters.

If you're dealing with young or new-to-LA agents, get them to dinner. During a friendly wine-laced meal, I find out what I need to know. I befriend the other agents to get information and set the tone for a positive exchange because regardless of what happens in this deal, I'll work with these people again. That's real estate, where the same 15 people sell 95% of the town. Sometimes, we make a deal to make a deal. We finalize this one and co-list one of mine. We're always recruiting for good cop/bad selling.

That said, everyone has a personal style. Find yours, play to theirs, and then throw them off. Study them. Learn them. Know them. You'll strategize more effectively. Know what to expect. Know what you want. Then get in their face and dig for the following:

- Do you have any offers? (They will tell you this.)
- How many? (They might tell you this.)
- How much? (Highly doubtful anyone would ever tell you this.)
- Are you representing any of the offers? (Important: If the agent is repping both seller and buyer, they'll want to make both commissions. In California, you must disclose if you represent both the buyer and the seller.)
- What matters most to the seller? Cash and financing? Rent back? How motivated is this seller? How can we make a deal?

This is a reconnaissance mission and every detail helps. If the other agent is young and inexperienced, I may have a younger agent make the call because I don't want anyone on the other end getting intimidated or defensive. I always tell the agent I have a client interested in their house as well as one other.

The "one other" is unknowable to the other agent and I've just inserted some leverage in a spot where I didn't have any a few seconds before. "Two houses" depowers the other agent and lessens the chance he or she will try to hardball me. I mean, come on, it's not like we run out of houses in LA. The shark knows there are many fish in the sea. I always sow seeds of doubt, hold facts close-to-the-vest, and hint at that I know something that is, in reality, still unknown. It's all leverage.

Know your goals. How badly does the client want the house? Know your terms – the financials, including offer parameters, market value, financing, inspections, and schedule. Your goals are tied to your client's feelings about the house. Ask your client: Is this a good house or a great one? Do you like it or love it? Is this the one you pray won't get away, or are there other properties you liked or loved as much or more?

Get a picture of where the client's emotions are. Take the client from Kahneman's System 1 thinking (fast and emotional) into System 2 (slow and analytical). Discuss every possible scenario, from acceptance to losing the house. Pad the landing. Often, it takes not getting a property to get a client to pursue another aggressively. Some gotta lose to win.

Remember the golden hammers you picked up during your interactions with the seller, the bits of essential insider knowledge? Google the owner of the property. Is there any worthwhile information there? Do you know the motivations of why the house is changing hands? The seller's situation should dictate how you offer. Money and its rate of flow to the seller will always be your two biggest hammers when buying a property.

Here's the thing. Every client who has ever lived is afraid of overpaying. And if they're whining now, just wait until they see your commission check. That's why I always do three things: first, I advise and reiterate to clients that it's their decision; second, I reaffirm my own expertise and interpret what the market is saying; and third, I set up the financial guardrails against paying more than the house is worth. If the client has a lender, that bank or financial institution won't lend more than the value either. If your clients are rich like mine, they are not as concerned with overpaying for inspections. If the clients are rich, they'll pay what they feel like paying and have the money to fix what they need to fix.

If the property is an investment, different questions need to be asked. These questions will determine the offer. What are the intentions? Flip or rent? Different laws cover each. What's the condition of the property? Can you get it up to speed, renovate it to meet the market with the money you have? Is it a good deal or just a buy? Keep in mind investing is much less emotional than a house to make a home in, or at least it should be.

If you want to make money in the rental market, my advice is to buy listings that have been around longer than the average days on sale in your market (DOM). You'll get a better deal. A quick way to think about it is, can you get 1% of the total cost in rent each month? That means if you pay $100,000 for the property, you get a $1,000 a month income stream, and so on. This will dictate your offer and you can use this model as a map in dealing with the other agent when making that offer.

Another way to parse it is by monthly payment. If you're in the rental business, you may be paying cash as you add to your empire. If you get a mortgage, figure out your monthly outlay of costs. Take your monthly mortgage payment, plus your property taxes divided by 12, utility costs, and a 5 to 10% contingency for repairs for tenants. Add those figures up. If you can rent the place for hundreds, or even thousands, more, do it. That's an investing snapshot, an easy formula to remember before you dive into the details in guiding the offer.

Sit down with your client. With their feelings in mind, start talking offers. Base the discussion on real estate facts now; take the emotion out of it. What's the right offer on this property and how do you get to it?

If there is financing, what's the client cleared to? If they're working with a lender, your client will have a firm threshold. If it's cash, there may be more room. Inform your client that sellers often weigh offers based on how the money is delivered. Cash is fast. Financing has a longer tail and lots and lots of paperwork. You can compensate for financing by sweetening the deal with other terms, but the cash usually wins.

Neighborhood comps are the touchstone of offers. Which houses – with the same numbers of beds, bathrooms, location, and equivalent upgrades – sold in the last six months within a mile radius? Drop the highest and lowest sales price (for the best and worst property), add the remaining "sold" numbers together, divide by the number of houses, and get an average. Next, calculate the DOM, and that includes all the time it spent on the market.

If a house won't move, there's usually a change of agents coming and it disappears and reappears on the market. Sometimes, sellers sit out a season if it won't sell. Be sure to know the full DOM. It's important to negotiations and can provide an important hammer. If the DOM is higher than the market average, you may get a real deal. If your client is full throttle in love, and the DOM is two days, welcome to the fast lane. If you're two days in and the other agent is already getting offers, go in strong and build as much sweetness into the deal as you can.

A word of caution: We'll go through all the ways to make a deal better without overextending, but we'd never want to overpay. If the DOM is on the high side, say 92 days in a 50-day average market, offer on the lower side of your comps. You may get a true bargain and will definitely get a counter.

The offer size should also reflect the market. In a buyer's market, the excess inventory provides leverage. If you're the buyer in a sellers' market,

I always advise my clients to offer on more than one house; hedge their bets and always, always have a Plan B (BANTA, best alternative to a negotiated agreement). Understand the market before offering or you're flying blind. Real estate agents obsess about the status of the market, and with good reason. It informs most every move a real estate buyer or seller makes.

Reconfirm the neighborhood and exact location of the house by making sure your information on them is up to date. Don't take anything online as gospel. All of the big online MLS services use the plans filed under the first building permit, even though they are rarely updated while houses are constantly being renovated and changing. Does the house border a green zone or an alleyway beside a mall parking lot? Is this location really good for the buyer who must commute? School needs? Lifestyle? Property taxes? Utilities? Use this in calculating your offer and be prepared to use this in negotiations.

Also, revisit the specific issues of the house. How old are the appliances? Are there any necessary renovations? How are systems, such as plumbing and air? These are the fixes that must be done now. List your client's immediate needs, estimate the costs, and take it off the offer. Inspections during contingency may bring more. The math tells you the facts of the offer. It's the rational process you use to get to the final number.

Your last act is that heart-to-heart with the buyer: How hard do you want me to fight for it?

I'm working with a young couple on their first house right now. Their parents are giving them the money to buy a house – all cash, $1.5 million, a pretty cool wedding gift if you ask me. We saw a two-bedroom house in Silver Lake on Wednesday, went back twice the same day, and they fell in love. I spoke with the seller and immediately began working the System 2 thinking. He wasn't going to entertain any offers until the upcoming Monday. A Google search of the owner told me he is an attorney, married, and they live off premises.

I initiated a strategy with my clients and decided to go in at full ask on Thursday, putting a 24-hour time cap on the offer. I never wait! I mean, why? Going in early doesn't have any meaning legally, but I've planted a flag to let them know my clients are as serious as hell. Besides, the seller has to respond immediately, and in the age of technology, that means immediately no matter where on earth they might be. As I said, this is a 24/7 job. It's my way of life.

My buyers then wrote a letter to appeal to the seller's heart. All of this is a risk but my clients don't have another half million in cash lying about. What we have is speed, cash, and full-ask. We came in early as testament to our intention. If these sellers want cash right now and someone who loves the house, our offer has a chance. If they call soliciting a counteroffer, we'll see what is possible. Remember, every counteroffer restarts the process and you're back in the game.

My newlyweds didn't get the house in Silver Lake. The seller wanted to wait and ended up with multiple offers over asking. Since then, these buyers have put in offers on two more houses. They have taken my advice to go in aggressively on multiple properties and it's just a matter of time until the planets align and they get a great house. Intelligent responsive clients really up the level of pursuit. They didn't throw a fit or get discouraged when they didn't get the first house; they rolled up their sleeves and went to work. Those are some great clients.

I tell my clients all the time, make an offer. Put the contingencies on and order the inspections. If you change your mind in the next 10 days or whatever the agreed upon time frame, or if the house doesn't pass its tests, withdraw the offer. You won't lose any money except for the cost of inspection, which is a few grand, nominal in the scheme of property purchase. As I like to say, "It's just the cost of doing business." If you're competing hard for houses in a seller's market, offer and don't stop looking.

INSPECTIONS AND CONTINGENCIES

In broad terms, the inspection covers heating and cooling systems, electrical, plumbing, termite, mold, foundation, roofing, drainage, structural, and more. The report sometimes will not cover issues such as lead, rodents, or chemicals and gasses. You must ask and no doubt, the cost of the inspection will rise. It's worth it though; anything is worth not buying a defective house.

Good home inspectors alert you to problems and assist in pricing out solutions. Say there are termites in the deck. If they're good at their job, they'll connect you with a good exterminator; you get the estimate and negotiate it off the final offer – that is if the problem is surmountable and your client still wants the house.

Now, with any offer, an earnest money deposit (EMD) is required as a declaration of intention. You have to put in some skin up front in real estate. Without this deposit, one buyer could run all over town, squeezing off written offers and taking great houses off the market, holding the market hostage. The EMD, like almost all things in real estate, can be negotiated.

In most markets, including California, it's typically 3% of the purchase price and it's held as a credit against closing costs and the down payment. If you're offering in a tough seller's market, the EMD may shoot as high as 10%; it's another way to create leverage when trying to win a house. If your client loves a house, however, the bigger the EMD, the better the chance for the offer. Nothing says "I love you" to a seller like money.

Also, you can build in an escalator clause into the offer. Hot markets require you stay out in front of your offers. That means, if you really want a house, you offer and have a strategy to win it over the other offers. Online auction sites such as eBay use the same escalator method, which means you meet the highest price automatically and raise it X amount whenever a higher offer is received. This continues until you reach an agreed upon threshold.

Remember, in a highly competitive situation, if you set a threshold above the value of the house just to get the house, you may have to pay the difference to the seller because the bank won't. If this doesn't get your offer accepted and your client is still in love with the house, you're going into sudden death, the final shoot out. Or are you?

In a seller's market, don't freak out and slap on an escalator just because, and then skip the appraisal to sweeten the pot, or you may end up with a property worth less than you paid for it. That's a real estate fumble on your own goal line. Use an escalator when the client is in love with a house and there are other offers besides yours. If you're using a lender's money, they flat out won't let you drop the appraisal contingencies. They don't want to be stuck with too much house either. If the house appraises lower than market, the seller must drop the price or you walk. Others may be all cash and stay in, but you walk.

Sometimes you need to stand strong. You make a "best and final" offer. Best and finals are standard tools for the buyer. You put together an offer based on your calculations on the value of the house as well as any terms you think will make the offer most desirable to the seller. You can put "best and final" on anything and then submit again after a rejection by the seller, so the term doesn't mean much, unless you want it to. I've submitted best and finals to be rejected and, if the client is in aggressive pursuit, I counter anyway. In a hot seller's market, standard protocols do not matter.

Now, never offer more than the house is worth in a best and final. It's a mistake unless you know you will long for this house forever if you don't get it. Don't get shook by using a best and final. Stick to the price you know is right. If you want to go over, go over. It's like the question "how much is this house worth" turning to "how much is this house worth to me?" Both questions are important. Only the buyer can decide – or a real estate agent with a heart of gold.

Enter Matt. We had a client, a dot-com billionaire, dreaming of a particular house in Pacific Palisades. He was relocating to Los Angeles to start a new business and would be relocating his entire staff. He was overpaying for the house he wanted by $2 million, which was a drop in the bucket for him. It was keeping my brother up at night.

I told Matt to drop it. That it was the client's dream home and the money didn't matter to him. Even after telling the client multiple times that he was overpaying by $2 million, Matt still couldn't let it go. He searched nonstop for a week and found the client a house he loved even more, even though it was $6 million less than the other house. The client bought it. It's not always about commission; it's about relationships. Now Matt is sleeping again and since then, two of the dozens of CEOs involved in his new endeavor have contacted Matt because they need houses. I suspect many more will call.

So, you never want to overpay, but how do you sweeten terms without overpaying? What motivates the seller? Is it just money or is time a factor? Are they selling because of divorce? Is this a move to start a new job? Is the calendar a part of the equation? Is this part of an estate that survivors long to settle? If they would like to stay in the house offer a rent-back deal. Let them stay rent-free for an additional two months after closing. The point is, negotiate. Make a deal. You don't know what is possible until you ask.

Real estate offers share a recurring theme. Most sellers are always going to hint at a world of offers about to flow in. Make sure you have proof or you're just going to bid against yourself. Don't do that. Ever. To concede small meaningless issues during negotiations is one thing – hell, let them feel like they are winning so the agent can look like a star to their seller – but don't offer more money. If you feel you're being played, retract the offer. There are just too many great houses to buy. When you find one, offer cash – if not for the whole deal, for as much of it as possible.

When in seller's markets, I suggest you go in with the cleanest of offers. Get cash, or get as much of the offer in cash as possible. Don't hang a bunch of contingencies on the offer and collapse the schedule of due diligence. A 14-day inspection period works, but 10 days is even better.

If you're wealthy and your attitude is that you'll fix what is broken because it's only money, skip some of the due diligence. A lot of my clients do. Outside financing slows a deal, but it's still the way of majority of real estate transactions in the United States are handled. Lenders slow the process because they are professionals who double check and move paperwork on all aspects of the deal.

MORE DEAL SWEETENER DETAILS

Again, negotiate and close any kind of real estate deal that you and the seller both agree on that doesn't break any laws. This is a creative business; find ways to the seller's head and heart. I've already described how cash payments, EMDs, escalators, and rent-backs can help sweeten the deal. Here are some additional points to consider:

Cash versus Financing

In a seller's market – that's places like New York, LA, San Francisco, and Dallas – we want to knock as many competitors out as we can with our first offer. International buyers mostly use all cash because a lot of them can't get a mortgage to buy in the United States. That itself has skewed the numbers of all-cash transactions. It's wild and crazy.

The majority of the all-cash offers are your fellow citizens, however, and you're going to have to match to win the property. The cash delivery is about so much more than the money. It's about freedom to do the deal immediately without lenders, and allow your clients to move on to their next home or investment.

Have your buyers contact their bank and make funds liquid. The bank then issues a "proof of funds" letter on bank stationary, signed by a bank officer, that you submit with the cash offer. If you show up with cash in the trunk, we'll send you back to your bank to do this. When buying all cash, we put in a rider that borrowed funds can flow into the transaction at a later date. Turns out our rich clients like to use other people's money too. Seller's agents never pick up on the clause, and it gives your client room to rearrange their money as they see fit.

Increase the Down Payment or Shorten Escrow

The standard down payment – at least one that doesn't require additional PMI (private mortgage insurance) – is 20%. In recent years, however, the National Association of Realtors found the national median was 10%. The down payment is held in escrow and will be applied to closing costs and the mortgage. On most of our major multimillion dollar deals you will see at least 30% down most of the time.

In California, escrow is usually 30 to 45 days, but any amount is acceptable if agreed upon by both parties. Shortening escrow is an attractive term for sellers with a calendar; they need to move and have probably already moved out in their heads. Collapse the timeframe as much as you can without undermining your efforts to get a great house.

Shorten or Remove Contingencies / Due Diligence

"Due diligence" involves the process of making sure the house is as sound as the seller says it is. If you're waiting for your financing, build it in to the contingency timing. Contingencies clauses usually involve (a) financial arrangements, (b) inspections, (c) shorter periods for due diligence, and (d) appraisals. If you order the inspection and appraisal immediately, you should be able to get it done immediately. The pros handling these matters are part of my Dream Team. I use them again and again. Hammer it out with the other agent.

Covering Closing Costs/Conveyances

Offer to pay for a list of expenses attached to the final processing of documents; title service, survey fee, recording cost, transaction stamp services, and so on. The buyer usually covers costs for inspection, financing, and attorneys, but if you can dream a different arrangement, you can negotiate it.

As a part of the offer, if the buyer wants to offer on any furnishings, appliances, chandeliers, outdoor furniture, and the like, do it now (provided it's up for discussion.) This point becomes especially necessary when dealing with international moves and second homes. I like to keep furniture separate from the deal and so do lenders. Besides, used furniture is often worthless in this game.

Set a Closing Date

If your money is ready and you know which inspections you want and when, set a date after they've been done and evaluated. If you don't find anything, close. If you do, begin negotiating fixes, new inspections, or other problems – or walk away. You've got whatever the time agreed upon in the contingency to make sure the house is viable.

AS FOR CURVE BALLS: PLAY BY YOUR RULES AND GET THE HOUSE

If your client truly wants the house – will die without the house – and the other agent comes back to you after "best and final" to reject your offer, bid again! Sure you're back in when you said that was your last offer, but who cares. Money talks. If you want the house, keep going back and get it. The seller can decline the other highest bid and accept your counter-offer. It happens all the time. Like I said, there's no loyalty in real estate, so don't expect it. Don't wait to make offers. Go back until you're heard.

As a real-deal "Hollywood" agent, it's also important for you to be aware of a few curve balls out of the playbook. Be ready to deal with one or more of the following scenarios.

When Sellers Won't Respond

Some sellers refuse to take calls, only communicating by email. I've delivered offers that sit in in-boxes with no response. Crazy, right? But sellers don't have to respond to an offer, no matter how it's delivered. If your client is in love with the property, keep working on the seller, perhaps sweetening the offer. Walk if you can't get an answer, and remember the seller's name. Should you bump into them again, turn their silence into your hammer by reminding them. A little guilt can work wonders.

Plan B or BANTA

Don't make the mistake of getting pulled off the larger arc of open, work, and close when in a ferocious seller's market. You might offer on two hotly contested properties and both fall through. If you've stopped the work phase of the arc, you are in a stall and about to start losing altitude.

Your BANTA is always the next property or the next one, or the one after that. If you have a buyer gassed up and idling on the tarmac, your job is to get them in a house they love just as much as the house that got away. You are responsible for always thinking about the BANTA and selling it to your client throughout the transaction. If the deal blows up, your next house ready to show is your BANTA.

Two Is NOT Better than One

My mega-wealthy clients don't worry about carrying two mortgages. They don't worry about mortgages at all. My other clients do. If you are in a house that hasn't sold yet, don't offer on another. First, if the seller has any sense, he or she will reject the offer immediately. You simply cannot know for certain when a house will sell.

We never accept deals contingent on other properties selling. The seller also doesn't know if the buyer has a competent agent or a good marketing plan to sell what they own. Why would a seller go along with this when there are other very real offers coming in?

If a seller wants to negotiate with you, anything the law allows can be arranged, including a right of first refusal. So why would a seller tie their own hands like this? The right of first refusal is standard contract talk. A buyer can submit a "contingency" offer that outlines the offer and terms based on the buyer's property selling. When it does, the offer goes live and the closing paperwork begins. A savvy seller will build a "bump back" clause into that contingency that says they'll take any other offer they want while waiting for you. A seller might also take a contingency to buy more time to sell, a hedge-your-bets technique.

Commission Breath/Desperation

It doesn't matter if you're buying or selling a house: If the agent or seller is desperate for money right now, it gives off a smell. People pick up on it like a shark smells blood in the shallows. If you catch a whiff of commission breath, you have a huge hammer. This agent is dying for a check and will do anything to speed up the close. Try a lower offer, all cash, with a quick close. See if that gets you the house.

Commission breath is a state of being for agents who do deals only when their bank account gets low. I can consistently get good deals on houses from them so I pay attention to their listings. It's a shame for their clients, but I must do right by mine. Less experienced agents get commission breath during the learning curve. (From the start, I banked half of everything I made. That money is the Scope that chases commission breath away.) Don't blow a close because you're desperate for a payday. Have some padding somewhere.

Now, go talk with your client, size-up your opponent, and make that offer! You're an animal! A beast! A shark! Be ready to adjust, adapt, and overcome! Negotiate! Give to get! Please your client! Win the battle! Close!

Chapter 24

GETTING AN OFFER

If you're repping the seller and you get an offer, you need contact every interested potential buyer who walked though the house – unless that offer is exactly what you and your client dreamed of. If there's anyone out there who wants to make an offer for a higher price, you have a very short amount of time to bring in it. Again, in the state of California, real estate offers have a 72-hour expiration date, so by law you have three days to accept or reject. (If you're working with me, however, it's 24 hours.) The clock has started.

Call other agents whose clients liked the house. See if they want to make an offer. If good agents hear they have an opportunity to make a buck, but are about to miss out, they'll get moving. That's human nature, and it's our job to create these pressured moments that demand immediate action.

You're at the table. You're ready for battle. You're ready to close. You're a killer and you already know. This is what all the work was for. Just remember: If an offer is unacceptable, you turn it away, and if you don't get another, it's back to square one. That's the business. You take it off the market, make any necessary updates based on all that buyer feedback, reshoot the visuals, and go through the process again.

Most people don't have that luxury, though. House sales are based on new jobs and schools, expanding families, and settling estates.

When an offer arrives, analyze it like a seller does. How close is it to list? Is it within an acceptable range of comps? What are the terms? How big is the EMD or down payment? Does a faster closing schedule have value? When does the seller need to be out of the house? Is the DOM high? Or is the DOM low and more offers will be on their way?

The legend of first offers isn't urban; it's real. First offers often land right after the first open house, and they come quickly from a buyer who fell in love with the house. Most sellers feel that a first offer will be followed by bigger offers, but it could turn out to be best offer the seller gets. Take first offers very seriously and advise your client to as well.

I always tell my clients whether I think an offer is good or not, but I never advise them to "take it" or "don't take it." Let the final decision rest with them. It's their money. People bid against themselves despite me telling them not to. Raise the EMD or down payment, collapse schedules, and negotiate furniture and appliance sales to the buyers. If the offer could be better and I'm not getting movement, I work the phones, provoking the fear of missing out (FOMO) in potential buyers and at the same time pulling the triggers of urgency and exclusivity – all this in the hope of starting my favorite real estate moment, the bidding war. God, I love bidding wars.

On the selling side, as I said in Part I, you can use triggers but it's my experience if someone is going to offer on a house, they offer. That being said, we pull triggers all day long. Every salesperson does. There are tiny triggers: "I need to hear back from you by 2 p.m. if you want to see this house." And there are huge ones: "This is the last house in the entire development and I have the first offer."

All the triggers may work, but you often don't know which ones. At the end of a long open, work, and close process, every trigger you use might inform the final deal. Here are a few that The Altman Brothers have used over the years with great success:

Exclusivity or FOMO: Is this house one of a small number of its kind? Say, "This is the last house on this street to sell; it's also the best. It backs up to a green zone and the developer used top-of-the-line materials to finish it out; yeah, this one is special for a special buyer." In the Hollywood Hills, my exclusive might be, "Are you kidding me? Keanu, Leo, and Beckham live within a few blocks. You live here and you're ground-zero rich AND hip."

Neighborhood of peers: For some buyers, their peers determine where they live or where they don't live. Say you are an executive for Whirlpool in Cleveland. I'm your agent and I take you first to the neighborhood where many of your peers live. I find this out through experience or networking. You say, "Wow! I can golf with Jim down the hall on the weekends!" or you say, "Screw this! I don't want to think of work on Sunday." As we drive a neighborhood, I might say, "The main homeowners are doctors, lawyers, and the university dean," giving a snapshot of education and income. Believe it or not, wealthy clients tend to be influenced the most by their peers. Other clients have different concerns, like money.

Urgency: This trigger speaks directly to real estate time and the need to move fast. Price deductions are a perfect moment to create urgency when you call all your most interested parties and say, as if each one is the only one, "I wanted you to be the first to know. We're dropping the price and it will not last. I want you and your client back up here."

Stack your showings: After the initial open house, take all interested buyers and, if possible, schedule them one after another for showings. You want them to bump into each other, creating a sense of desirability and competition. Nothing creates urgency like an offer. That urgency dies on the sidewalk if the seller isn't ready.

In the next chapter, we'll discuss multiple offers as well as counteroffers. But for now, get the offer, get on the phone, and get another offer! Get three more offers! Get five more! You're "Hollywood"! That's why you're client hired you! Conquer the deal! You were made for this! You're a winner! A warrior! Be ready to adjust, adapt, and overcome! Negotiate! Give to get! Please your client! Win the battle! Close!

Chapter 25

MULTIPLE AND COUNTEROFFERS

You may have seen me deal with multiple offers on *Million Dollar Listing LA*, walking out of a dinner, standing on the sidewalk and shouting into my cell phone while I have the other agent on hold. For me and every real estate agent I know, bidding wars are a rush, a high. I live for them. You should, too. Learn 'em. Lure 'em. Love 'em. Leverage the hell out of 'em and close.

Now I'm going to break down multiples and bidding wars from the seller's point of view. Buyers should just flip the advice and, in a seller's market, they will have new insight into how to hit a seller's hot buttons, get 'em squirming, and win the house.

Getting new bids almost always involves more cash, less time, and some crazy terms. The highest bid, preferably all cash, with the shortest closing schedule is usually the winning offer. Usually. For the buyer, however, leverage lies in the contingencies. If the house doesn't pass an inspection, say, the leaky roof is deducted from the price – that is, if you still want the house. If the appraisal deems the house is worth lower than its list price, that's more leverage to lower the offer. If the buyers need financing, the lenders won't approve it for an overvalued house. The process of selling real estate – more open, work, close – has built-in trip wires so buyers and their lenders don't buy defective houses unaware. Be aware of this or these landmines will blow up in your face

For buyers, counteroffers mean you are in the fight. It's a good thing and one you must power through to win a house in a tight market. Don't stand down. If you love a house, make an offer because you just never know. If you aren't an all-cash player, sweeten the deal. Go back to the previous two chapters and see what you can work into your offer and counters. Know your boundaries. How high will you go? Stand firm. Fight. Have a walk-away number. This is important. Many get lost in the passionate back and forth of war. There blood gets pumping in the heat of battle and they overpay for a property.

No matter which side of the table you're on, buyer or seller, remember, you are a team. The goal in any negotiation is not winner take all. It's creating agreement that benefits two or more parties. You discuss every move with the client and build strategy together. You are their heart and their head; you know their needs and their intentions. Your client's money is your money. If they're happy in victory, you're happy in victory.

Listen up, some real estate agents watch offers float by, acting on the one the seller likes. These agents will never work for me. Why would you do all the work to get to the negotiation and not work the most exciting part of the process – the close? Your job is to get the best price and terms for your client. That's it. That's the goal. Play the offers. Work the deal.

NEGOTIATING ON THE CLOCK

To master working multiples is to truly own the shot clock. Once it's set, it's yours. Play it. Hit the buzzer beater. You've got 72 hours. Maybe 24. Maybe two. Love that clock. Manipulate the hell out of it. Which deal do you want to keep active and which do you want to reject? Are you watching your top offer in every round? Are you expecting more offers? Who else can you call?

Multiples require great organizational and analytical skills that turn on a dime. Don't shy away from it. It's why I suggested you practice negotiation on the smaller deals. It builds confidence and develops negotiation as habit. Negotiation must be your breath, the reason your heart beats, the blood in your veins. You can approach multiples any way you like, but there are standard identifiable moves when you have more than one offer in front of you. I like #2. It's why my clients keep coming back. It's why I make money. Big money.

1. Just accept whatever offer the seller likes best.
2. Issue counteroffers to one or more buyer.
3. Ask all buyers to resubmit "best and highest" bids.
4. Adjust the price and look for more offers.

Different circumstances call for different moves; but #2 is your go-to, the one most likely to set up a real bidding war. Remember, always be respectful. It's not just a general rule of life and Game-Time mentality, but it's good business because you don't know which, if any, of these potential buyers you'll have to go back to.

No deal is ever the same and no deal is ever easy, even a "small" one. I would also make the argument that there are no small real estate deals; every one impacts someone's life. In a seller's market where multiples are standard, it is my experience they tend to move like this:

1st offer: It's often lower than list since the buyer has no idea if anyone is interested in the house besides them.
2nd offer: This one tends to come in closer to asking.
3rd offer: This is usually a strong offer, at ask or over list, because the buyer really wants the property.

Every offer is under the clock and will expire. The same is true of every counteroffer. You must keep track of it all, opening, working, and closing each offer as you work with the client to reject it or move it forward in the rounds. Every time a new offer is written up and submitted, the terms must be examined quickly and understood.

During multiples, real estate time gets vicious. It's killer. The clock ticks, the weapons drawn and fired. If you were stressed getting your house launched, this phase will test your might. In all 50 states, there's no law that says a seller has to respond to a real estate offer. It can just sit there to signal a seller's rejection. If you're trying to buy the house, you have to submit and then counter, and maybe even counter again, to get the seller's attention. To get into the game, a potential buyer might break the silence with a higher bid or larger EMD money. So pay attention.

I was working on a sale in the Pacific Palisades, a rare one-acre double lot that backed up to the Riviera Golf Course. If you can manage to get into the Riviera, it's a $350,000 initiation fee to golf with the likes of Adam Sandler and Larry David. The landscaping around this house was wild. I'm talking Amazon forest wild with a large pool and waterfall. The owner's rep had me come to the property and told me they wanted to list it at $9.5 million. "That's too low," I said, "I can sell it for $12 million." He took me up on my offer. "If you're so confident, I'll give you 30 days to bring me an offer at that price. Otherwise, you lose the listing."

After a handful of showings, it was apparent the house would not sell to buyers as is. The house had never been renovated. It was a tear-down. I had to get to my BANTA pretty damn fast if I was to meet the deadline. I had to pivot and reset my strategy in an afternoon. As the great fighter Mike Tyson said, "Everybody's got a plan until you get punched in the face."

I decided on a builders' auction. I invited them in, set up the forms, and took offers. I was completely pumped about what I saw. I had a solid $10 million offer come in. During the event a builder called me. He had just heard about the house and wanted in, but was out of town. I said, "Bro, I have so many offers in hand, a week from now won't cut it. The house will already be sold by then." And I hung up.

Later, I met with the seller's rep. I should have guessed his mood when he said, "I can't imagine how you got me to drive from Beverly Hills to the Palisades on a Friday." I tried to loosen him up a bit. "Are those shoes comfortable without any socks?" "Yes, my shoes are fine, Josh. Where are the offers?" He was all business. I presented what I had, certain he'd be pleased: one of the offers was over what they orig-inally wanted to set the ask price at. He was not pleased. "Josh, you told me you could get more. Therefore I told my client, you would get $12 million, and $10.4 million is not $12 million. You know, Josh, you haven't done what you've said you were going to do and now I have to fire you from this listing."

I remember going cold so I'm sure the color drained from my face. I couldn't believe it. "Starting at $12 I assumed $10 would be the settling number and I got more than that with $10.4 million." "If that was the thinking," he said, "then $11 million would be the number. Come on, Josh, we know this game. My client might go for that, but $10.4 million is not our agreement. You said you could do $12 million in 30 days."

I had one last play and it was a 1,000 to 1 shot. "I had one builder call during the showing. He was out of town and couldn't bid sight unseen, but I told him we couldn't wait. Let me give him a call." I got him on the phone and told him, "We've gone to best and final. $11.2 will get it for you but I have to have an offer in writing in the next hour."

A few beats passed and I received the text message. The seller's rep and I had an offer from the guy for $11.2 million and we closed the deal. I was ecstatic, jumped into the pool in my suit, the really expensive one made of the finest threads in all of Italy. Closing-wise, this was a close call. The shot clock can be a bitch. The sweetest part about that deal is I caught it all on camera on *Million Dollar Listing LA.*

NO RULES? USE HAMMERS FOR LEVERAGE

Multiple offers and bidding wars are the Wild West; the rules are no rules.

Now, as I'm working the phone issuing counteroffers, I might say something like "tell your client if he can afford X, he can afford Y." I go back through my notes on potential buyers and look for hammers. I call the two with tight timelines first; both have kids starting school in August. "This house is going," I tell the other agent. "If your client is going to offer, I will need X by Y," and I start adding more players to the bidding. I might find notes on a buyer's reaction, call the agent and say, do you remember your client who toured 408 Thrasher? She melted over that view and kitchen; it was perfect for her family, she said. I have offers and I want to give you and your client a heads up. I want you guys to have a shot at that great house." You keep stoking the fires of FOMO, exclusivity, and time, nudging all parties toward war.

Once multiples arrive – even if it's two – know your exact response time. Know the shot clock and the play, when you need to deliver. As more come in, you need to analyze quickly and decide if any of them is the one. It's all about price and terms.

Evaluate the price in relationship to the terms. How much higher or lower is it than list? How do the offers fall in line against each other, lowest to highest? Does the highest have the best terms? Or does another offer have those? What is more important to the seller? What does your seller need most? Cash?

Do they need out of the house immediately or in two months? Are they trying to buy another house? Have they submitted a strong financial picture to the seller along with their offer? Great credit and a job still matter in America. Do they want contingencies? Appraisals? Inspections? Are there caveats attached?

Setting a cut-off day and time for offers isn't always necessary, but helps to keep things moving. It can be nudged and even ignored in a lot of cases so not to lose potential bidders, but set the clock to play the clock. In a high-end market, powerful people make power moves. Their pride and reputation depend on it. They can and they will pull rank. Still, sellers will most often choose the most attractive offer no matter when it's made, so if you lose a house as a buyer, ranting and raving about rule breakers will do you no good. There's no loyalty, remember?

I had a penthouse in Downtown LA. It was $4 million. We got a ton of offers. We countered a ton of offers. We went back and forth for days. Right as I was about to accept one of them, another offer came in out of the blue with a higher price and better terms and stole the property away from everyone else. So after all that work, here came the dark horse that robbed the whole lot.

Bidding wars can continue as long as the seller wants to keep going and buyers are still submitting offers and counters. As you open, work, and close each offer, use any one of these ten hammers for leverage:

1. **Time:** Hook the shot clock to everything you do to nudge deals forward. Some of it is already wired into real estate transactions by law, but in real estate, speed matters. You can jump over time to show enthusiasm or wait until the last second and knock out other offers. Think strategy.
2. **Boundaries or parameters:** If you're the seller, a boundary might look like "no offer below X." If you're the buyer, it might be "start at X but do not go beyond Y." In the speed of multiples, you move within these walls and, if you're the seller, you nudge them upward while sweetening any terms you can. The buyer, once their financial threshold is reached, needs to have a plan with contingencies to sweeten the deal.
3. **Your playbook:** The playbook, or "the narrative," is your reasoning for the values you've set on the property and the deal. Don't get swayed from what you want by other people's play calls. If you aren't completely clear about what you want, what you need, and what you will accept, people will attempt to get you to agree to their narrative. Don't. If you've pitched this house as the last four bedrooms in the most family-friendly neighborhood in town, you are still selling that value.

4. **Token concession:** At the beginning, I always make a goodwill concession on a point I don't care about. It sets a mood. Give to get. I usually come up with the concession during the work phase when I'm listening for hammers to exploit. Because we know energy begets energy and close begets close, if you start the ball rolling with great energy, it might set a tone for better, more engaged, and open negotiation.

5. **The win-win:** The cliché "win-win" is classic negotiation-speak for "You get what you want, I get what I want." Call it integrative bargaining. For the win-win to work, you need to visualize and pitch how it benefits everybody. Nudge all parties toward agreement. "We're looking for something between X and Y" is an easy way to push/pull an interested party into your line of thinking.

6. **BANTA or Plan B:** For the buyer, it's always another house. For the seller, it's another buyer. Keep your eye on what you need should the deal fall through. (The playbook, #3 above, is the reason you keep such fine notes; if you have to go back to the beginning, it's a lot easier if you can reconstruct what has already happened and pick it up from there.)

7. **Power:** Everything from what you wear to what you say should speak power. Dress power. Select your words and strategize power. Use silence to get others talking, because information is power. If you're an experienced, well-known agent dealing with a young, newer-to-the-market client, that's the power of experience.

   The most powerful tool of all – so powerful it gets its own chapter at the end of this book – is the walk-away. Project to your counterparts that *you don't have to do this deal*; let them worry you'll bounce. That's true power and success. A great example of power is on the reality show *Shark Tank*. The row of investors sits mute while entrepreneurs dance in front of them as fast as they can. It's set up like that to show who has the power.

8. **The over-ask:** Go in asking for more than you expect to get. You never know, you just might get it. It also allows you the power of saying what it's worth, and buyers will feel like they got a steal when you say "yes" to their price. Usually though, your counterpart will push for a lower price and you'll end up at your expectations. Say the buyer wants the furniture. Your client puts the number $20,000 on it, so you ask for $30,000.

9. **Friction:** Two forces moving against each other create friction. That's you and the other side of the table. Disagreement is the foundation of democracy, free markets, and most marriages. It's a good thing. Don't shy from it.
10. **Knowledge**: I can honestly say agents miss points in the offers I submit at least 50% of the time. They're just so focused on a final number. Terms matter. It's why I told you to build endurance and game-time mentality. Don't lose focus here because the war is almost won. Read everything, even the fine print, on every offer, and then read it again. It's what you miss that'll kill you.

As you issue counters, work with your client on them, keeping expectations as even as possible. As you go over your attack plan, strategize where you want to take the sale. I have some clients who are willing to push all players to higher numbers, thereby accepting the risk of driving some away. Others hit a certain number, get pumped, and call it a day. Here are the six most useful hammers while negotiating counters.

1. When you issue counteroffers, you'll have a big hammer with **urgency**. Everything already has a legal shot clock attached (72 hours).
2. Your **boundaries and parameters** lie in front of you – the lowest to highest offers, as well as the number you hope to achieve. How do you move from one number to a higher number?
3. The **over-ask** might work for you; counter higher to get to the price you want. The over-ask is based on the belief that the buyer wants the house and will counter your counter somewhere in the middle.
4. You can approach an offer with the **win-win** strategy, pulling a particular buyer to the head of the pack and closing the deal. You can attempt to nudge any buyer higher with the win-win.
5. Never shy from **friction** and disagreement. It's the bedrock of free markets and democracy. We work our own side of the fence, finding a point of commonality. As we know, that's usually money. None of this is personal; if you don't meet resistance, it's an anomaly.
6. People just get too crazy around real estate. Money and pressure under time make people act weird. The more **knowledge** you have about all the players – your seller, the house, the neighborhood, the market, the buyer's agents – the better to anticipate multiples and counters.

Learn these lists as if your career depends on it, because it does. You're "Hollywood" now. Be "Hollywood." Be a beast. Be a shark. Embed hammers in your brain so when the battle goes down you'll be in the fight, counter after counter, no time to think, only to react. Know what to do and do it. Fold these moves into your style. Style, I love that word and everything about it. The Altman Brothers are "style." I am "style." You are now "style." Let's move on and talk style.

Chapter 26

PSYCHING OUT BUSINESS STYLES

I'm the Shark, all class in an expensive suit. I project confidence. I'm aggressive, but I'm also a chameleon who pays attention to all players of the game. People's business styles fascinate me. It's like watching a wildlife show on the Discovery Channel. Some agents are all boast and bravura, thumping their chests as if they are gorillas, while others attempt to draw you in, all affection and excitement, like puppies.

Don't confuse their styles with their abilities to close. The deal is the deal no matter how it's delivered. But understanding the difference between style and substance is key to the Altman Close.

Sometimes, as I'm getting to know my counterpart, I use the mirroring technique. I might be running around and an agent yells, "Josh, I'm sending you an offer on Wilshire today, man!" I yell back over my shoulder, "Thanks, man! Can't wait!" I've matched the off-hand tone and we both keep moving. I might encounter another agent, a "dot the i and cross the t" type who says, "I'm submitting an offer by 4 p.m. I'd like to hear from you immediately." With that style, I might push back a little, reaffirming leverage. "I'm looking forward to it. Lots of action on that house" and walk off. I like to leave that type hanging.

If you study business styles, there turns out to be a label for just about everyone. Labels are bad in negotiations because if someone knows your "type," they'll turn it against you. So it's easy, don't have a "type." Move to the moment by turns conceding what you do not care about—to get what you do.

If you recognize yourself in any of these style descriptions, mix it up. Let go of as many rigid characteristics as you can identify. "Style" blinds businesspeople and their deals suffer because competitors like me are watching and strategizing how to play off their weaknesses. You may sit across the negotiating table from any one of these types or someone who works for them. If you know what the boss is like, often you can predict the style of the employee. Here are the most obvious types:

The Royals (I Win – You Lose)

This is a person who must have dominion over all the lands, including yours. Both Steve Jobs of Apple and Bill Gates of Microsoft fit this description. They invented the damn kingdom then crowned themselves.

Rulers are notorious for not listening and I rely on that deafness, even though their clients are probably unaware of it. It's a highly competitive and often destructive position to take when working toward agreement. Breaking down an autocrat takes strength. You know your parameters like you know your own bed. Use your silence (let them run their mouth) as a time-out to reassert your power and re-engage. Authoritarians want to run the clock but that just isn't how the world works. It takes two to forge an agreement.

The Self-Defender (You Win Some – You Lose Some)

Self-defenders often work for Royals or OGs (see below). All that authority beats them down, makes them concede too easily. If you get this reputation, watch out. Word spreads and you will have trouble during future negotiations.

The Passive-Aggressive (I Lose – You Lose)

Passive-aggressive types usually work for the Authoritarians and want to avoid any issue that is daunting or could land them in trouble. Working with this type, you'll have to take on the responsibility, which is great, while making them think they're helping shape it, but that can piss you off. If you want the deal, though, passive-aggressive people are a fact of life.

The Intellectual (I Win – You Lose)

You see the Intellectuals coming from 50 yards. They have a big stack of documents in their hands and want to hit you over the head with paper. They bring piles of comps and analyses and photographs and reports hoping to overwhelm you with information. Don't be fooled. It's all smoke and mirrors. Nothing should pull you off your position. These types can come off as real estate nerds, but with many of them there's aggression behind that fancy approach. Be forewarned.

The Parent (I Win – You Win)

Now that I'm so deep in this market, I don't meet this type much anymore. It's an offshoot of Authoritarian, only much nicer. They'll pat you on the back and say, "When I got started . . ." So, if Authoritarians are the parents and I'm the child, I play young and dumb and then slay them with a burst of strategy and experience. Play to the situation and the person, but don't be fooled into giving up a position you want to keep.

The Democrat (I Win – You Win)

This is the integrative bargainer, the person who runs business based on building consensus and agreement. Democrats are great bosses and usually highly productive negotiators. But sometimes you have to agree to disagree and the Democrat above all wants agreement. Sometimes, it's just not possible and there has to be some friction to get where you need to get.

The Collaborator (I Win – You Win)

With the Collaborator it's all "you and me against the world, so let's make a deal that's easiest and best for us." If a deal comes to a standstill, you really may need to collaborate. But this is a bad look for real estate agents: It's not about us; it's about our clients. If you put your clients aside, are you really an "agent"? I say no.

Mr. Nonchalant (I Win – You Win)

I work frequently with a builder, and man, do I love the guy. He is so chill it's as if he's asleep. Sure I've seen him flip out a time or two, but it's rare. You'll know if you're negotiating with a nonchalant type – they'll yell a number at you as they disappear into the restaurant, laughing. You stand on the street scratching your head. It's like chasing a feather in a cyclone and can be completely maddening. The nonchalant must be pinned down and confirmed for everything.

The OG (I Win – You Lose)

Most markets have real estate OGs, the hard-ass "old gangster" types, the "I've seen it all so don't try it" agents who consistently enrage colleagues but can get huge results for their clients. These types exhibit a single emotion, usually anger, and tend to be unyielding and vengeful. They will remember everything that happens and will carry it forward in future dealings. The OG does not worry about "good relations." It's war with no reconstruction.

Why do these labels matter? I outline these "types" so you can recognize them and negotiate to their weaknesses. Your main modes should be any one of the collaborative win-win styles, moving into competitive mode for negotiation points that really matter to you. Be careful of losing focus and getting dragged into extremes – remember the air-conditioning unit that almost wrecked a multimillion-dollar deal? That's where people get locked into dogfights over nothing at all. Your leverage is your refusal to do it.

We've had a lot of fun over the years coming up with ridiculous labels and there's a lot of truth in the jokes. If you come up against the same small group of agents every year, get to know their style and work with it. You also need strategies to work around or blast through their nonsense. To combat any intractable behavior, you need to:

- Be clear about what you know and don't know, and if you sense the other agent is covering something, you are probably right.
- Use the word "no." It works.
- Hold your position and let the other agent explain their reasoning.
- Hold your position and explain your reasoning.
- Break pissing matches by moving on to another point and circling back around to the disputed one.

It's just human nature to want to get away from someone you don't like, but you've got to hang in there. Negotiating can be a well-executed rush or a frustrating shit-show of clowns. You may outmatch your counterpart by 10 years of experience or be facing a genius closer. Don't blow it just because you want to get away from whatever is facing you across the table.

It's also human nature to learn through pain and negotiating with difficult people. That's what you'll remember. The more experiences you have, the more competent you get at contentious closings. When the dust settles and you're outside of the deal, analyze it. What parts did you negotiate well? Did you miss anything? How should you have dealt with it? Did you get the number you wanted? The number you thought it would be? If you didn't, why not?

Did you negotiate other terms that made the client happy? Was anything you said or did particularly effective? Did you use time to drive the deal? FOMO? Or was it sheer sales, full of nudging and pulling?

Real estate is a small, gossipy world no matter where you buy and sell. If you consistently show a weakness during negotiations, it gets out. That's why you look back at the deal. Was there any money left on the table anywhere? Did you go far enough to find the right offer? Do the contingencies satisfy your seller's needs? Did you run tight counteroffers, getting back to everyone on time and with respect? Did you sustain the bidding as long as you could? How were your communication skills? Did your client understand everything that was going on? Did you function well as a team? Are there any deal points you gave away that you wish you hadn't?

You want to constantly close gaps in your negotiating style and abilities so that other agents don't develop "recycled" hammers against you. If the local industry views you as soft on putting down earnest money, they will recycle that hammer and beat you over the head with that low EMD. What if you now have a seller in a do-or-die situation, in need of moving money immediately, and they want to take this one good offer now? You will have a hard time raising the EMD without another bidder.

Your closing reputation is constantly tested in negotiations and there's nothing more surprising and annoying to the other side than when you don't fall for one of their moves or better yet, use one of theirs on them.

Years ago, I used to face an older agent who loved to call me "kid" at the top of his lungs. I was just beginning to build the business and was sensitive about being new to the market. And, it just pissed me off. I started calling him "Pops" at the top of my lungs, and it's funny how quickly it went back to first names and indoor voices.

Living the examined life in business isn't a path toward happiness; it's the commuter's lane to bigger paychecks. I please clients to make money. That's my goal. That's the prize. I open, work, and close. Analyze each deal and improve anywhere you can. I keep a file of all my sales for the last year. Listed by address, I can give you every detail of how we did it.

That's the Rain Man of LA Real Estate talking, but holding these details in my head provides a huge advantage. I remember what worked and what didn't. I keep moving what works forward and self-correcting quickly as I do the next deal and the next and the one after that.

Real estate closes are not just about numbers. Anyone who has watched *Million Dollar Listing LA* knows real estate is about drama. Owners have intense bonds with their homes and hate turning them back into houses. Buyers have dreams about the future and how they want to live.

We race the real estate clock to launch a product to maximum fanfare into a highly competitive market, trigger offers and counters into a final best and close it out. No matter how tight you've wired your deal, every moment of the closing arc is full of emotion that can explode a deal in your face. That's why every agent in this respect is always Agent as Therapist. Remember, the goal is to open, work, close. The goal is the get the best deal for your client. Drop the ego. Play the game. Play the person. Close.

Chapter 27

PUTTING ON THE POKER FACE

Here's the thing: In negotiations, in business, in life, people piss off people. Suck it up. Put on a poker face. Remember what your goal is – to negotiate the best deal for your client, close deals, and make money. Not to duke it out in the parking lot.

Like I said, when it comes to money, a pressured shot clock, and someone's livelihood, people get weird. They get nasty. Suck it up. I don't care if you're cursed off, rudely dismissed, or get a drink thrown on you. You're a mature adult trying to close a deal. This is business. Suck it up: no emotion, just a poker face. Make money. In the words of my father, "Don't believe in the person, don't believe in the project, believe in yourself. Act accordingly."

THE ANGER HAMMER

Imagine that every time you lose your cool in negotiations, a big shiny hammer appears in the sky and comes hurtling downward, right toward your head. (Let's not confuse this anger hammer with the golden hammers of knowledge we use to wield power in negotiation, but if you can get a handle on the anger hammer . . . well, I'll get to that later.)

Emotion, especially anger, is weakness at the negotiating table, and if you can't find your poker face, buying and selling real estate is going to be hard for you. Don't whine, don't bitch, don't pout, don't curse, don't get angry, don't pace, and don't storm out. Shit happens. Not everyone is as respectful as they should be. Know this going in and be prepared to let it roll of your back with a smile. It's the job.

At the same time, where there are people, there are emotions. Even me – an animal, the Shark – I am still human. Many times I have wanted to launch across a table and beat the hell out of an agent or a client, but what kind of way is that to act? That's high school shit. Like it or not, we're made of emotion. What matters is the type of feeling and how hard and loudly it is expressed. If you let emotion override your mission – which is getting the best for your clients – you have failed.

When it comes to emotion in a real estate deal, you have three choices: (1) feel it and express it, (2) feel it but don't show it, or (3) program it out of your system.

You never want to be in the position #1, wearing your hammers on your sleeve. Save the venting for home if you must.

As for #2, card players aren't born with blank faces. They cultivate their look over time. Hell, most even wear sunglasses to hide their eyes. Here's where the poker face comes in handy. If you need to, practice. Seriously. Silently say "poker face" and let your facial muscles go slack. Train your muscles to relax on command. Develop muscle memory. This is a proven science. Through repetition, you train a muscle to move or not move in a certain way. A baseball player may practice a shoulder rotation 1,000 times before using it in practice, another 2,000 times before throwing in a game.

When you get a good blank face going, look your counterpart in the eye. Keep your body loose and relaxed. Your voice should be neutral and focused on the facts at hand. Breathe evenly. The poker face is easy to master and you'll find it effective in many situations beyond the negotiating table. It helps you relax in general.

Programming the emotion out of your system, #3, is a little more difficult to pull off. It takes experience. If you've been in this situation before and can reason your way out of it with confidence, you'll have built a winning strategy with a crystal clear mission. You are relaxed and clear-headed. Maybe you meditate, pray, or have assessed a situation and placed yourself in an "I don't care" zone with eyes on the prize.

What about me, you ask? I lift at the gym every morning. Not only does it work out stress by releasing endorphins, the accompanying breathing is a meditation. I come out of that place ever day, completely oxygenated and ready to work, calm, cool, hungry for a deal.

The greatest center of negotiation research is just outside my hometown, at Harvard's Kennedy School of Government, which teaches future leaders diplomacy and the art of avoiding both war and famine all over the world. Their work saves millions of lives. The business and law schools have legendary programs as well and they've created a large body of research, still changing constantly, on the effects of emotion when trying to forge a deal. The greatest offenders in the emotion category are anxiety and fear.

Until the last century, transactional deal making – that's buying and selling to you and me – was studied primarily through strategies and tactics. Researchers studied how you squeeze the most out of every deal through offer and counteroffer strategies, skimming over the fact that humans were making the transactions. Researchers finally began to study the impact of emotion, but it was more the "impact of mood" and how positive and negative outlooks affected final outcomes.

In just the last decade, reams of data have been generated on the impact of specific emotions, which has given negotiators lots of hammers to throw as well as strategies to get their own feelings under control. I've seen a lot of emotion over the years and I've learned to use it to my benefit.

Fight or Flight Modes

If you watch closely, you can link physiological signs shown by your fellow negotiators to emotion. Sweaty palms and quick replies might signify anxiety, a sure sign this person is in "fight or flight" mode. This is evolution. Way back when we lived in caves, a tiny part of the brain was dedicated to identifying predators. Saber-toothed tigers, velociraptors and other man-eaters like sharks wanted to eat us alive. This part of our brain perceived the threat and would kick into action. Still does. That's your "fight or flight" center and it lives in your head in an area known as the "lizard brain."

I have been in more than one negotiation where I thought, "Oh yep, they got lizard brain." From there, you know that this negotiator will want to windup quickly and flee the table, so now you have a hammer in hand.

Throw them a life preserver in your benefit. "We could wrap this up now if you'd just . . ." and see if they jump. You've given them an out of the process. Meet your demands and they're free.

Anxious negotiators often have low confidence levels and deliver weaker first offers, which means in most cases they are weak negotiators. You come in low and weak, your offer probably won't win the day. Your entire business will suffer. If you can't overcome it through experience and changing your behavior, you should get a different job.The anxious also seek advice and affirmation from other parties. Remember, in the words of my wife's yoga teacher, "Leaders don't need cheerleaders!" I've even seen non-leaders ask advice from the person negotiating against them, and they often can't discern who is on their side and who isn't. You can "coach" the non-leaders with comps, presenting your narrative, your playbook. For a shark like me, the anxious are fish in a barrel. I plant an idea in their heads, one in which all my deal points are accepted, and I assist them in thinking it was all their idea.

You never know where bad behavior is going to flare up and screw up your deal. It can come from other agents, potential buyers, and even your own client. It's a minefield of low-self esteem, ego, emotional baggage, and need. And, well . . . fear. Sellers worry about two mortgages and buyers worry about being homeless.

The more you acknowledge emotion and understand it in yourself and others, the better real estate agent you'll be. That's it. Suck it up. Poker face. It's just one of those jobs where you've got to read people and the charge they give off, especially your own clients.

Anger is aimed at someone or something while anxiety is turned inward. Anger is the fight part of "fight or flight." Some negotiators feel it's useful. They see the negotiation process as "me against them," a zero-sum game or a fight for the biggest piece of pie. It's not.

Keith Allred, a former professor at Harvard's Kennedy School of Government, is the man when it comes to anger and its affects on negotiation. He studied it for decades and didn't find many positive affects. Angry negotiators foster conflict, reduce gains, decrease cooperation and cause every bad feeling to escalate. They may not remember their clients' needs as well as neutral negotiators do, and that's because the emotion disrupts memory. They also get their offers rejected more than those who park their emotions at the door, suck it up, and put on their poker face.

The body language of anger is usually the give-away. Be aware of this in yourself and others. Most people don't walk into the room in full fist-clenched melt down. Look for the signs. Tight lips and tense facial muscles are signs of stress and anger in another person. A furrowed brow and locked stare might make them seem even angrier, maybe even a threat. Diffuse immediately. Suck it up. Poker face. Play nice. Diffuse. This is business.

Stay Grounded with Emotional Intelligence

"Emotional" intelligence lies in your ability to observe and diffuse situations where anger is stopping your ability to get a deal done. The chip-on-the-shoulder negotiator must be dealt with, but how? If they are like the grenade that stops deals, you need to make sure no one pulls the pin. People snap. They go nuts. Help them not or use it against them. I find a pointed question usually quiets things down.

If a guy walks in all pissed, I try calling it out politely, maybe with a slight stance. "Are you angry at something or just trying to throw some shade in hopes of intimidating me? Can't be done, friend." The fact you saw it and called it first gives you leverage. Naming something gives you power over it. But be careful: Use innocent questions, not labeling statements. Just like telling your lover in a heated argument, "You're so angry. Relax and calm down," it could escalate things quickly. Be aware of this and be ready.

A pointed question also makes it more difficult to lie. If you suspect the anger is a show to cover something, pointed questions will draw it out or you are sitting across from one hell of a liar. This same type of intelligence helps you manage the feelings of others, creating the environment you like best at the table. You can try humor or empathy. If the other person continues to be pushy and overconfident, it's time to show a subtle bit of anger from you. That usually induces a healthy amount of fear to get things moving.

You can also label your own emotion instead of just apologizing. Try saying, "I just get so damned passionate on behalf of my clients." It puts an entirely new spin on it, doesn't it? The point is to run the show by presenting emotion in the context of how you want your counterpart to see it.

Positive emotions affect negotiation as well. Since there is usually a long run-up of meetings and showings and strategy and phone calls before a closing, each point of contact is a moment to keep the process and the feelings positive. If and when you sit down at the negotiation table, the environment is alkaline, not acidic. No venom necessary. Remember that your job is often to act as therapist. Be cool. Be respectful. Be firm if need be, but acknowledge the other person. Be empathetic and understanding in most cases.

Matt and I have a 90-year-old client who is about to move to assisted living. The builder who is buying the house wants to start work immediately. Carrying costs are high once escrow closes, but the elderly woman can't move into her new apartment until a week after the close. Even in the frenzy of getting a new build started, the builder sat down and we renegotiated a five-day grace period so the woman doesn't have to see her trees ripped out. She will reduce the purchase price $10,000 so that she can exit her house with it whole. I admire the builder. He chose empathy and it meant the world to her and her children.

Empathy will help keep emotional charges out of the air so you can move forward. The more you understand your counterpart's motivations and goals, the better you can align them with yours and work out a deal. That's the idea right? Closing a deal? You're goddamn right it is. You're "Hollywood." You're a closer. Close.

Now, I'm a baller and damn proud of it. I'm a shark, a closer. It's integral to the hustle. What I am not is a wannabe tough guy – the ones who flex for show and are full of it. Fake thugs. That's a potentially dangerous deal-wrecking animal. True tough guys keep their cool. I get my high from making deals, from making money. I'm not going to ruin that for a pissing match with a fool.

KNOW THE CLASSIC HARD-BALLER MOVES

Before I can tell you how to respond to "hard ballers" – and I deal with them constantly in the celebrity world of Los Angeles – let me isolate their moves and catch phrases:

Extreme Demands with Slow Concessions
The Behavior: A seller might demand a buyer raise the EMD then not respond to earnest requests for, say, appliances or large outdoor furniture.

The Anecdote: Keep your eye on your BANTA (next house, next buyer) and know your bottom line. Insist they respond to your request or your BANTA kicks in.

"My Hands Are Tied"
The Behavior: Hard-ballers will claim they have no choice just to get you to stop working a deal point; it's on someone else, they'll say.

Since it's not always possible to know if they are telling the truth or are full of shit, make the whole game real.

The Anecdote: I say, "Well give me the phone number of the decision maker. I'm trying to make a deal here." You'll find out quick if it's crap or not.

"Take It or Leave It"

The Behavior: Nonsense. The entire purpose of a negotiation is a back and forth, an agreement of some kind. The "my-way-or-the-high-way" life isn't the right one for a real estate agent. Versatility and cooperation will get you better outcomes and much bigger checks.

The Anecdote: Focus on your deal points and keep on mission. Insist on negotiation. Sit through the nonsense and restate your point, working toward a deal. This is usually all bark and no bite. They want a deal. You know it and they know it, otherwise they wouldn't be at the table.

Concessions without Counters

The Behavior: I love these types. You make an offer and they immediately start pushing for more, trying to get you to bid against yourself. This is an easy one.

The Anecdote: Say, "Issue me a counter, please." Hang up.

The Huffers, the Puffers, the Liars

The Behavior: Some real estate professionals love wild exaggeration, veiled threats, insults, and warnings to do what they say. That's BS. If you feel ruffled, get up for a minute and reset the conversation. Better yet, ignore them.

The Anecdote: Call them on it. Tell them you need the back-up information on their wild claims and that you don't do insults. Tell them you'll come back when they have control of themselves or to cut the shit and keep moving toward a deal.

Wannabe tough guys are often covering for what they don't have. That's confidence, respect, and knowledge. Sometimes, being a wannabe tough guy is an outgrowth of commission breath, desperation. None of their moves are particularly good or skilled, but to do the deal, you've got to try and get them in line.

USE CONFIDENCE TO GRAB THE HAMMER

As for confidence, there's the general confidence a person may or may not carry, and there's calculated confidence. I talk about this all the time. If you've done your research and worked your deal, you have no reason to walk into the final phase of a property sale feeling anxious and angry.

This is a transaction, a transfer of money, not a date to the prom. You have a clear objective and there is no reason to get involved with anything other than that. Do not engage the angry. You grab the hammer, control the time, and let them simmer down. Got an OG still seeking revenge for something she didn't like in 2013? Do the deal with her and if you have to, call her out every step of the way. In negotiations, the ones who remain even and keep their cool get the best result.

Alright. You've now marched through multiple offers and a war, closed, and thrown back celebratory tequila shots with the other agent. Your focus is on two new active opens as well as the continuous passive openings of two speaking engagements and a podcast. Your mind is on new clients, facts, and figures, and looking back over a deal isn't appetizing.

I say you should and you must. Just as you go over the details of the negotiation, analyze the emotion around major points. If your opponent expressed anger, what did you do? Did it work? Did you suck it up, poker face? Were you successful in getting the negotiation restarted?

What about you? Did you lose your cool over anything? What was it? Do you have any understanding of why? I'm not asking anyone to enter Freudian analysis here, just think about it. Does another agent really hit your buttons? Do you have any idea why? Are you going to let it affect your career?

You've seen me on TV. I've had to keep my cool many times. As a result, I make money. That's the best revenge. Do the same. That's the job. Remember, this is chess, not checkers. I'm only here to close deals and make money. What's your goal? Are you "Hollywood" or high school? Be a professional.

Can you power through your emotion with a poker face? Predictable emotions help your opponent manipulate you. Don't show weakness in war. If you run hot, you will be pulled off rational points. You'll fall victim to misdirection as they stir your emotion over something that doesn't matter to cover up something that does. Emotion is not always weakness, but not understanding it is. Act accordingly. Take notes on your own reactions and if the feelings get in your way, use your rational mind to neutralize.

If you hit negative emotion around something or someone, run it through your System 2 thinking. Your feelings are real but did the event happen the way you saw it? Did you see all of it? It sounds stupid, but all day long we run around making assumptions that aren't good for anyone. Remember, even in the mob movies the hothead is always first to be buried in the ditch. If he's the Alpha – the Joe Pesci who makes it to the last act – he still ends up getting tossed in the bay.

Don't be the hothead. If you constantly feel worked over by a situation, figure out how you can stop the feeling. Empathy helps. So does understanding. Suck it up. Poker face. Close. Make money. Keep your cool. Keep your head. Be a pro.

Chapter 28

THE WALK-AWAY

Now here's the part that really gets people shook, the true headache of selling real estate. You're a shark now. Your mere presence intimidates.

Sometimes all you have to do is swim by. The fish scatter. The seals find the nearest rock. The bathers flee for their lives. If they stay in the water, they're constantly checking around, unsure what to do: all because you came and went. They may come running after you, begging for you back and meeting your terms, but it may not matter to you anymore. They're not ripe enough to eat. This is a superpower. This is the walk-away.

In order to be in full control of your movements and emotions, you need to be prepared to leave the deal and move on. Why would you do that?

First off, you don't sweat one deal. It's not going to make or break you. There's many fish to swallow and there are many reasons why negotiations crash. So, why pull the walk-away? The contingencies were not met.

The inspection report triggered a drop in offer. One of the other parties wants to lengthen or shorten time frames, and on and on it goes.

Don't assume anything in negotiation. Always ask pointed questions, especially when someone is hard-balling you, acting the jerk, or is unforthcoming. Try to get to the bottom of any statements that ring false or contradict what you know. Business isn't personal. It's a transaction, and you can do it rough and stupid or play it like a true professional, smooth and in control of your game.

The science of a deal is in the numbers, the art in how you manage yourself, your clients, and your opponents. If you are relaxed, know your facts and approach the negotiation with a win-win (integrative bargaining) attitude, you'll get where you want to go, deal-wise. No doubt. So, what in God's name would ever make you walk away from a table you need to sit at?

For some buyers, their agent hasn't helped them jump from System 1 to System 2 thinking at the right time. The client's "love at first sight" feelings have come and gone, the honeymoon over, and they are no longer sure of the house. They haven't applied any critical thinking to the buy. They're lost, stuck, overwhelmed, and adrift. They second-guess themselves and pull the offer. Maybe their agent didn't hold their hand during the shift to rational thinking earlier in the work phase, the way you now know how – the "Hollywood" way.

But most often, the walk-away is a break between a buyer and antagonistic seller. The inspections come in. The seller minimizes the buyer's concerns, the old "It's never been a problem before. We're not going to pay for that." The request for fixes spooks them and the deal breaks. They refuse to negotiate. You give it your best, and then *you* walk. Now, they're screwed.

Strangely, more real estate deals are terminated over aggressive, angry behavior than lying outright or by omission. People almost expect lies, thinking others are always trying to get over on them. Like I said, people get weird. Hostility, however, is a consistent deal-breaker in real estate. That's the positive and negative charge again.

You repel people with anger and attract with cool, calm, confidence and optimism, ready to negotiate a good deal for all with an upbeat mood. You came to close and that means to make everyone happy. When people get shook, making people happy can be impossible to do. You try to chill them out with your many tactics, your give to get, but if they can't get control, you'll always face resistance.

Now, as for points of no return, every journey has one, a point at which, if you continue, you cannot turn back without supplies running out. For Lewis and Clarke, it was the Salmon River. They mapped it out beforehand and knew that if they crossed it, they were cut off from home. A deal is the same way.

You're ready for the game, for the battle. You know the field. You know the players. You know the clock. You have a goal. You have a playbook, a narrative, a plan all mapped out to achieve your goals with and for your client. Part of that map should show the walk-away as the far boundaries of your deal. So what is it for you, what's your Salmon River?

It should be the number, the walk-away point, where the deal is no longer beneficial to your client. Know that number, your boundary. Walk into every negotiation with that number in mind. What are your key contract points?

Say your buyer is in a time-sensitive position. They need to move for a job or kids and now the seller wants another 30 days. Is that a walk-away? Is it on to the BANTA, the next house? You and the client should work through your offer parameters beforehand. Communicate. Hash it out. Be completely clear on the points you can let go of and what you must have. In the spirit of win-win, you should be able to get there. We all know, however, sometimes that mountain is just too high.

My first walk-away was hard because the money was so big. The second I announced I was walking, I felt a massive rush of satisfaction and calm. The developer was a constant problem. Matt and I did the listing meeting and perhaps we were a little too persuasive. As we did our due diligence on the guy, he's pounding our phones every hour of the night and day. "What about this? What do you think of that?"

Suddenly it hits us. This guy sucks so much air out of the room he could kill our business. Not literally, but I've got 40 other listings on my desk at the moment so why would I do this? The answer is I couldn't. I wouldn't. So, I didn't. Early in our career when we needed money, maybe, but now, why do it to ourselves. He also had so many emotional needs it would have killed Matt, the hand-holder. I can't lose Matt.

The house has still not sold over a year later. This guy's infectious. Oh yeah, by the way, it was an $62 million listing.

There's this one agent in LA, Matt and I call him "Magoo" because he's like some cartoon character that blows up no matter what you say. We take bets on how long we can go without making him angry. I owe Matt $20 for the last meeting; the guy lost it 17 seconds in. He takes everything so personally it's a mental health issue. He's harmless, but we always walk. By the time you say something and peel him off the ceiling, it's taken double the time to settle an issue.

Time is that thing we don't have much of. The shot clock's ticking. When we're flowing, it's a rhythm we don't want to disrupt. Our value is our talent, our experience, and our energized hustle. We protect it because if we can't function at 120%, our goals suffer. We wouldn't rise above the rest as we have been.

If you are contemplating a walk-away, factor in its affect on your relationship with everyone involved. Who are the people across the table? What do they mean to you? If you do not reach agreement, will the relationship be harmed? Are these businesspeople who understand it's not personal, or are they over-invested sellers insisting on the illogical and the impossible? If you walk-away, will you threaten any deals in the immediate future? The long term? How are you going to feel about yourself?

If you walk, be prepared to reset your strategy and re-launch the listing. Since all of this took you away from the market, you need to climb atop real estate time and move fast here. You need to prep all for battle on double-time. It's another reason we take such detailed notes during the work phase. We might need those notes for the walk-away. There's so much leverage in the details; knowing you have it makes the negotiation and the walk-away so much easier.

HOW TO WALK AWAY

The thing about the walk-away is how you do it How you walk matters more than if you walk. There isn't a deal in the world that can't be rebuilt somewhere else. Part of a successful professional life is delivering difficult news like a grown-up, a pro. If you are going to walk, explain your position, thank everybody, and tell them you look forward to working with them in the future – then go. It's much easier earlier in the process than later, so pull out as soon as you know it will not work.

The goal is to allow all parties to face each other again without a grudge, no drama, no beef. It's business. It happens. You're proud of how you handled yourself. If they can't get over it, that's on them. You'll work with someone else. Otherwise, it's a new day, a new deal. Let's make it work.

As agents, we usually have to work with each other again and again and again, so it benefits us to keep it cool, respectful, and professional. We're always watching the clock and the walk-away devours time. We don't want to walk away, but when it's necessary, you have to. Beyond price and terms, an overly difficult client or counterpart sucks days from the calendar. We can't afford that.

We may outlast most in our efforts, but there comes a time to cut losses before more time gets cut. Sure, some clients need more hand holding than others, but only you can decide when it is having a negative impact on your other clients. Don't spend so much time on one deal that you lose the next. Your work piles up as you feed a client's insecurities and boom! Opportunity passes you by.

If you want to close it like an Altman, build the walk-away into your strategy. It's fail-safe, not a go to, but if you get there, you have it. If you run passive and active opens constantly, you cannot afford to be taken off the line for one deal. You have other clients and other commitments. If you are like me, you have employees. Interrupt the circle at any point, it starts to wobble and you'll need a massive correction that will kick your ass. Get tangled up with a deal for too long and you might have to close two or three quickly to make up for the lost selling time.

Our motto is to not quit, to stay in the game, but those are games worth playing. Know the difference. In caring for a client, don't forget to take care of you; keep your paydays coming. A major factor of the walk-away is a strategy to restart the work phase. If you've worked the Altman Close, you have the notes and know the people you can go back to ASAP. The sooner you get the energy going around a listing, the faster you'll restart after a walk-away.

Again, it's business and you should view the walk-away not as failure, but a reset. It's a tool, so use it if you need it. To be effective in the marketplace, or life for that matter, you've got to shake it off. It's just a part of the process. You can't sweat every deal. You're a baller. You don't need to.

After the walk-away and your analysis, repair anything that needs repairing, if you can. Fix it. Keep in good graces. Depending on the circumstances, and I don't do this for jerks, I wait for some time to pass and then give the other agent a call. The tone is loose and friendly and I invite them out for a meal or drinks. We can talk it out if we need to, keeping a bridge from going up in flames.

Humor is always a great healer. One agent was eating Fritos when I gave her the walk-away news so I sent a case of snack packs with a note "Here's to hoping it will never happen again." She immediately called laughing and we co-listed a great house in the hills together.

The walk-away is the most important part of the Altman Close. Without it, you are working without a safety net. If you fail to reconcile a buyer and seller, you fall through the floor, taking a horrible deal that diminishes you professionally and financially.

The walk-away protects you, your client, and your ability to make a deal, the real estate trinity you must keep in balance to be the most effective professional possible. You're a closer. Recognize what you can't close or what will take away from your other close. Try to make it work, but before you get to deep, pull the walk-away. Keep swimming.

Now, remember you're a killer, a beast, a shark. You don't clench up when you spot the walk-away. Its urgency has forced some awesome deals in my office. You have to get creative. You have to adjust, adapt, and overcome. Open. Work. Close. You've set up for this. Your playbook is already full of what you need.

Just thinking about the walk-away blows some agent's minds. How can you work on something for so long and then wreck it in an instant? Easy, I say, if you must. Experienced agents know they have the goods to remake the deal. There's calculated confidence. Communication is key. It is your go-to position with all clients. I never had a client tell me I called too much.

If it means calling a client with bad news, do it. Build something positive. Have a BANTA, something to offer. Have options. If you don't, you lose time and will be further off your game, under the shot clock. It's not life or death for you but it is for your business. Every time you talk about a listing to anyone, make detailed notes, track the information and refer back to it constantly. Know it. These are the "facts" of your deal. Everybody who loved the house, didn't love the house, felt it was too small, felt it was too big. Sit down with your client. Analyze, strategize. Open, work, close. Find the fix. It's there. You're a ninja. You've set up for it. You're ready.

Chapter 29

BE A SHARK: EAT, SWIM, DEVOUR

In Phase III of the Altman Close, the last act of the drama, the offers come in fast, fierce, no time to think, only react. The shot clock ticks down and you make moves on pure instinct, pure gut, all heart. Phase III moves like the Grand Prix. This is where the professionals step up, taking every offer and counter and working it upward into the highest, the best. The close races by in a blur.

But you're good to go. You're "Hollywood." You're researched and prepared. It's Game Time. You know what you want and you know how to get there. The walk-away is your own planned reset because you know what to do. You're a professional. You're a beast. You're a killer closer.

That's why I love my nickname. Sharks got to keep moving and everyone knows it. If you sit at my table, my eyes watch your every move. I break you down. I analyze all that has been done and said through every phase of the open, work and close. I know exactly what I want and what I'll give up to get there. I'll walk away from anything and restart a broken deal in minutes. I move that fast.

I'm a self-made millionaire who's lost everything and recovered. My skills are superior. I'm cool, calm, collected, confident, and calculated. But my teeth are sharp. There's always another house and there's always another client. I've set it up that way since the open. That's how I run each deal. That's how I run my business. "I'm Hollywood." I plot my strategies. I call my plays. I'm my own coach because I'm a superstar for my clients. I go to war. I win battles. I please. I close. I make money. Use the Altman Close and you will now, too.

Read on. Check out Part IV and see for yourself – a few "plays" from the Altman Brothers playbook.

Part IV

PLAYS FROM THE BOOK

Chapter 30

PLAY #1: DAMN, THE STUDIO HEAD'S PISSED

A big-shot studio head has been a long-time client of ours. We sold him a house that listed at $35 million to start but had slowly dropped in price during the year and a half it was on the market. It came all the way down to $19 million. We ended up getting it to him for $14.5 million, a smoking deal since we were able to negotiate $5.5 million off of the asking price. He bought the house and it's super-exclusive.

The studio head is all about privacy, like many of our clients are now. Often we sign NDAs. About a week after he closed, it came out in the media that he bought it. In our business nowadays, there's no way to block that; one contractor comes up, tells a friend, and it's news. So, he calls us up and he was pissed. I know this not just from his voice, but because he said "I'm pissed! People know, and I didn't want anyone to know that I bought this thing! Sell it!"

The privacy thing wasn't our fault. We never talk on our clients when doing a deal. We can't. We won't. Maybe he was driving up to the property and the paparazzi were following him and put the two together. The guy's gracious and he knows how Hollywood is. He didn't blame us, but we still caught the brunt. In real estate, no matter what, the agents are always to blame first.

Now, the kicker is when we feel a deal is good, we always tell our clients "This is a great deal, if you ever want to re-sell it, you're gonna make money on this." You know it's part of the sale, so when you say things like that you have to honor it, but it's a little harder to do only one week later.

"Alright, then," he says, "you said I'd make money off of it, resell it." We had to back up our word or potentially lose a big-dog client and a great guy. Matt and I were like, "Shit. Now not only do we have to resell a property that we already sold and everyone in the world will want to know what's wrong with it, but also we have to sell it for more money than we just sold it for so he doesn't lose money." We had to pause on this one, just for a second though.

Fortunately, the Altman Brothers have reach. We priced it at the previous MLS asking price and put it back on the market. We called a list of clients. We showed three people right away and thank God, the third person who came in paid $16.5 million. We ended up making him, after our commissions, about $2 million on it. It was a tough one, but it ended up being a win-win.

We set ourselves up by negotiating so strong on the buy-side that we protected our client and ourselves on the sale-side. We were prepared. We had to adjust, adapt, and overcome. We had to open, work, and close the same property twice in a 90-day period by the time escrow closed. We did it. It's part of the game. And we're the best.

Chapter 31

PLAY #2: THREE CLIENTS, ONE PROPERTY

When Matt and I got called up to a house for a listing appointment for a property that had been on the market for six months, we realized they were dropping their current price and their current agent. We paid attention to the shot clock, anticipated the changeover, and scooped up the listing. We were psyched! "Oh my God," I said to Matt, "This is the biggest steal."

With every property we think is a great deal, we always jump on the phone and tell our clients who have the money, "Hey, you gotta see this now!" At once, Matt and I got on our cell phones and called every client we knew who invested in this price range and had the money to close. We got through three calls, not expecting everyone would see the property on the spot.

Rarely when you make this kind of call do you get more than one client available to run up to the property then and there. This time, all three of them said "Wow, that sounds great. On my way. " All three showed. All three offered. We were then screwed and sweating this big-time. They were all our clients and now all against each other. How do you play that and please all?

To sell real estate, you have to be a shrink, a therapist. We are shrinks to all of our clients. We have brought families together. We have seen families ripped apart. It's the game. We deal with people in some of their worst times ever – grieving after the death of loved one, or going through divorce with babies stuck in the middle. But we also deal with clients in some of their best times ever.

If you think being a real estate agent is just about real estate, you're 90% wrong. It's 50% therapist, 50% realtor, and that's why Matt and I work so well together. We are each other's yin and yang. I'm the Rain Man of Real Estate and Matt's the emotional roller coaster. Matt will hold someone's hand from A to Z and really invest in the relationship, while I'm more the numbers guy. The Shark. In short, I sell houses and Matt sells life-long friendships.

It's a killer combination and I recommend a similar partnership for any agent. In the end, the property became a bidding war.

Always be upfront and honest when in a deal with your own clients. Matt and I decided to tell them exactly what happened. Believe it or not, they were all very cool and laughed about it. They trust us. We had taken the time and effort to build those relationships. They believe in us because we believe in them.

It's just how the game of real estate works, and as successful investors they all got it. They understood, and the property was worth more to one of them than it was to the others. I guess you could say the universe handled that one. I guess, actually we did. We just guided the deal along being respectful to our clients. One got a house and the others got state-of-the-art Altman Brothers concierge packages, aka Rolexes. Please one, you please all. It was just advanced Game-Time mentality.

Chapter 32

PLAY #3: THE MIDDLE MEN KINGS

Another time, a big client calls and says, "Hey Josh, I wanna buy at the beach in La Jolla." Our answer? "No problem."

The key is that all these deals that we do, about half of them a year are made from nothing. They are deals that most agents would overlook, but we never say no. So when people say, "I wanna buy a house in Colorado," what's our answer? "No problem, I got the perfect guy in Colorado, let me set it up." We're kings of connecting people and of being middlemen. Because of that, we are constantly making money when and where people think we can't.

I called up the agent and said, "I have a client who wants to buy in your territory. I know you usually pay a 25% referral fee. I have a bunch of agent contacts in your area and they pay me 50%. I'd like to start a referral relationship with you and I'll give you the same 50% when you send me a referral in my neighborhood. Now, I will give you this, but I want 50% of the deal if he buys anything."

To be honest, I didn't have any other contacts that were giving me 50%, but hey, I'm making deals over here. It's part of the game. Consider it listing language. The La Jolla agent accepted, but the client wasn't exactly sure if he wanted to buy there or if he wanted to buy in four other places, so I did that with four other agents, just in case, to cover all my bases. The client ended up buying one of the La Jolla homes and we got that deal. We made $100K off of it, and so did the other agent. One phone call was all it took.

The client loves us. The other agent also loves us. We now pass clients back and forth repeating the same formula. Matt and I brought people together, did little work, and everyone won. We continue to win, just on introductions we pass along. That's the kind of reach we have. That's the mindset. We try to say "no" as little as possible. We work as a team. We share. We close. It's easy money, and in this business that's hard to come by.

Chapter 33

PLAY #4: THE MOST EXPENSIVE GARAGE EVER SOLD

W e represent a guy we call the Ultimate Salesman. It's not what he sells, it's what doesn't he sell. The guy's a hustler. I mean the man has a hand in everything. He's a professional at all times and the most successful car salesman I know.

Anyway, the Ultimate Salesman calls me up and says, "I want you to find out about this garage." I say, "What are you talking about?" He says, "It's a one-bedroom with a 25-car garage." I had to laugh. "Of course it is."

It ends up being this awesome garage by the beach. The guy has an incredible car collection he has worked hard to build over the years. So I get why he wanted it, but never in my life have I strategized so much on a deal with my own client. The two of us would bounce off ideas for hours on how we were going to get this garage down from $10 million, a non-negotiable price, to $7 million. The replacement costs alone were more than $7 million on this property, and you could never rebuild it again because of the updated building-code permits for new construction by the beach.

In real estate we talk about how time is not our friend. But on this deal, time was our friend, for once, for a couple of different reasons. It's just something in real estate you have to keep focus on, time, the shot clock.

A unique property can be either a really good thing or a really bad thing. That means that 99 out of 100 people are either going to love it or they're going to hate it. So he was more like the one in a million type of buyer. We held a multi-month negotiation, far beyond the norm in real estate negotiations, which usually last a week tops, maybe two.

The plot thickens. During the negotiation the Ultimate Salesman says, "You know the owner of the garage offered to take me out for a ride in his classic Ferrari," because they're both major car guys. The Ultimate Salesman was reluctant. "I don't wanna do it because I think it will mess up the deal. What if I say something I don't wanna say?"

I spoke from my gut before my head could even formulate the words. "Actually, listen to me. Go and become best friends with this guy because he's going to give his friend the best deal that he'll be able to get."

He needed a little nudging, but there's no harm in making a new friend, and the friendship doesn't have to be built solely on the need of the house. Yet, it's a smart play. The guy had offered to take a drive knowing the Ultimate Salesman's interest in the property. So, our guy spends the next 60 days really befriending the owner.

They actually did become real friends. Eventually it got to the point that it wasn't about the money anymore. The owner wanted the Ultimate Salesman to have it because he was his now his friend and this way he knows that it's in good hands. After that, we got the owner down from $10 million, non-negotiable, to $7.25 million. It was a steal. We call that a grand slam.

This is all about closing and negotiating. There is something to be said about getting people to let down their guards in negotiating. There are so many different approaches to different styles and different cultures. So many people can be a part of it. It's not just you as the agent. In this case we directed our own client toward a further benefit for all. We were friends to him and he became a friend to another. Sometimes, it pays to be a good person and a friend, especially when it comes to a record-breaking sale of a garage.

I attribute our success to creative techniques like this. I'd say we probably have the lowest rate for losing clients compared to other real estate agents on the planet, and that's because Matt and I become so tight with our clients that we can literally send them to go look at houses without us and never worry about someone else stealing them.

Now if someone ever walked into one our houses without an agent, call it a grey area or not, that person is leaving that house as our client. I don't know if it's because we just get so heavily involved in them, their life and their family, or because we offer so much more in the deal than just real estate. It's business. It's friendship. And people like doing good business with good friends.

Chapter 34

PLAY #5: THE PARAMEDICS OF REAL ESTATE

"Whatever we hit, we destroy." We were selling a house to a movie star. We were in escrow to sell the house for $6.5 million. We represented the house, not the movie star. It came down to the ninth hour. He was supposed to lift contingencies, but his house overseas, which he was selling, fell out of escrow. And he had been planning to use funds from that deal to close this one. Now, most people would say the deal's dead. It's done. But we revived it, CPR real estate.

We found out the buyer had a big movie coming out a few months later and would be getting a huge payday, so he was good for the money. My clients who owned the house owned it outright. I said "Guys, we have no other offers, but I have a way where I can not only make you $6.5 million, I can make you $6.8 million," and they said, "What do you mean? How?"

I said, "I need you guys to lend this guy some money on the house. I want you to be the bank and offer 8% interest on the money you lend. Over the next 24 months, you'll make $300,000 more than you would've made."

I mean the deal was already cancelled, flat-lined, dead, but we reopened escrow the new way. We got the money back in and closed the deal. It's all about reviving the deal, being creative in pressured moments like this one.

There are many different ways to close. You've got to think outside the box and do CPR on the deal. Call us the "paramedics of real estate" – just another aspect of being a "Hollywood" agent in the Altman sense. We save homes. We save deals. Remember, Matt and I are just two punk kids from Boston. In the words of Sylvester Stallone, well, of Rocky in *Rocky IV* – "I guess what I'm trying to say, is that if I can change, and you can change, everybody can change!"

Chapter 35

THE FINAL PLAY: CONFESSION

If there's one message I can you leave you with, it's the following: Up your game. You have the tools right here. You have the heart in you. You're a fighter, a boss, a closer.

The Altman Close is based on an understanding of a real estate shot clock, on getting creative, and being strategic to get the best deal for your clients. The shot clock moves more quickly as you move toward conclusions, and you've got to keep using the clock for optimal efficiency.

Your days are filled with running passive opens to generate new business and flipping them hot as they engage with you and your listings. You're planning product launches, open houses, and broker's opens and working local vendors to get the best prices. Know when to drop the price and how maximize the moment, reaching out to potential buyers and recharging the sale.

In our first 10 years, as the Altman Brothers were becoming successful, we worked for our clients, we worked on their schedule, no matter what. They'd call, we'd drop everything, and we'd run. I think since then we've gotten to a level where we can say no to a client, "I'm not available right now." For the first time, that's a reality for us. We're more our own coaches, but we had to fight to get there and we still have to fight to maintain. But we have clout now.

I still put my clients first, but I respectfully put them in their place when I know it's best for them, more than I ever have, and they respect me not being a "yes man." But I earned this. They still know I'm in the game for them. They bank on it and I deliver. Matt and I just have the luxury of being a little more on our own clock now, due to our success. Our goal was always to make our own hours in order to spend more quality time with our families. And now we can, all while still selling a half a billion in real estate this year, working smarter, not harder.

We've found it's better to be smart as well as honest. We admit to people that we're at a stage in our game where we can be completely straight up. We're not just telling you what you want to hear so you'll go with us, and then risk that six months later you'll be disappointed. We're up front and we'll tell you your house is worth X. We are experts. We know what we'll sell it for within a certain realm. If you want to list it with what we suggest, then we're your agents. If you want to list it higher, then we're not the agents for you.

But we'll be nice to that someone and say, "We'll give you a call in a few months if it doesn't sell. We hope you sell it, but if not, let's talk when your contract expires." To turn a listing down, and then be the second agent on a deal, or third agent, is sometimes best. We just did that with a house called Bliss Canyon. We ended up getting it fourth, or maybe fifth. We were able to get it to the appropriate price of $30 million after being on the market for twice that amount with the previous agent. It's a different hustle for us, now.

In real estate, negotiations start from the day you meet your client. If the client is selling, you negotiate to get to a price point where the house can sell. That's the first negotiation. Then the next negotiation is with the stagers, and then on to the showings. The next negotiation is with agents who are writing the offer. And then there's the contingency period where you do your inspections, then your commission, and then you renegotiate your commission.

You do dozens of negotiations within a real estate deal. You negotiate your commission 10 times. People always feel that the real estate agent is making too much money and that they should throw in if they care about the deal, whether to the seller or the buyer. Be strong. You're worth every penny.

Still, my clients know I'm in it for them. Besides being with my wife, daughter, mother, father, brother – or watching the GOAT win another Super Bowl – there's nowhere I'd rather be than at the negotiating table, deep in Phase III and about to sell a $20 million house to a guy I met 10 minutes ago from a seller I opened at the gym that morning. I'm a real estate agent. I'm "Hollywood" in the Altman sense. I'm a baller. I'm the Shark. I close – the Altman Close.

THE END

ACKNOWLEDGMENTS

I want to thank my family first and foremost. Heather, this one's for you, baby!

Mom and Dad, I love you so much. Thanks for teaching me that everything is negotiable.

Matt, it's always a pleasure breaking real estate records with my big brother. Thanks for being our clients' therapist in every deal.

Lexi, you are the reason I am no longer a workaholic. I can't wait to come home and give you hugs and kisses every day.

Lisa, thanks for taking my side all the time when Heather tries to negotiate against me at home.

Sidney, Sara, David, and Edith – I miss you all so much and will never forget you. The best grandparents a kid could ever have.

My dogs Diego, Lucky, and Brady – you guys always gives the best licks.

Tom Sykes, way to be a closer. Thanks for taking this home to the finish line.

Michael Broussard, you are the best book agent around.

To the Wiley team – thanks for believing in me. Richard Narramore, I couldn't have done it without you. Thanks for everything, it's been a pleasure working with you and your team. Let's sell the dream!

Everyone at Bravo, NBC, World of Wonder, and *Million Dollar Listing LA*, thanks for allowing the world to see how I close and negotiate deals.

ABOUT THE AUTHOR

Josh Altman is one of the most successful real estate agents on the planet, specializing in the luxury housing markets of Bel Air, Beverly Hills, Malibu, and the Hollywood Hills. Josh's clientele consists primarily of A-list celebrities, professional athletes, business leaders, and high net worth individuals from around the globe. Josh and his brother/partner Matt have sold over $3 billion worth of real estate, including the most expensive one-bedroom ever sold for $21.5 million. At any given time the Altman Brothers have over $1 billion in active listings.

Along with his brother Matt, Josh created the Altman Brothers, (www.thealtmanbrothers.com), a one-stop shop that provides both buyers and sellers with their exclusive white-glove VIP treatment. Josh is known for its ability to listen and understand his clients' needs, allowing him to continuously deliver above and beyond their goals and expectations. His personable and professional character allows Josh to build and maintain solid relationships, which explains why his business has grown mostly from referrals and repeat clients.

Since early in his career Josh has always been heavily involved in all aspects of real estate. While many know Josh as a high-profile real estate agent, few realize that he had found enormous success as a real estate investor as well. Josh has quietly built a fortune buying and selling real estate with several of his best residential flips making him a profit of over $1 million each. Josh now has a strong passion for teaching others how to achieve success in real estate and believes that anyone can follow in his footsteps to change their life and financial future through real estate.

Due to Josh's impeccable track record of success, he was offered a starring role on BRAVO TV's *Million Dollar Listing Los Angeles*. He's currently filming season 11. His dynamic personality, humor, contagious energy, and love for the business have made him one of the most sought-after speakers on the global circuit. His unique background and rags-to-riches story allows him to connect with all ages, whether he's lecturing at universities and college campuses around the country or to the most demanding executive board rooms. With over a decade of experience and his personal success in real estate, Josh Altman has become a household name when it comes to high-end real estate. The breakout star of *Million Dollar Listing LA* has brought excitement back into the real estate business.

Despite his busy schedule, Josh still finds time to give back to his community and is very passionate about volunteering his time and money to support numerous charities and causes. Josh grew up in Newton, Massachusetts, and attended Syracuse University, where he was a kicker on the football team. While he was at Syracuse, the team won the Big East Championship two years in a row playing both in the Orange Bowl and Fiesta Bowl. After college Josh did a short stint in New York City before moving out West to pursue his dream of real estate. Josh has lived in Los Angeles since 2003, and currently resides in Beverly Hills with his wife Heather and their baby daughter Alexis.

INDEX

A

Ali, Muhammad, 26
Allred, Keith, 180
Altman Brothers Company
  about, 9–11
  branding by, 68–70
  close systems developed by
    application of, 209–210
    basic phases of, 14–15
    method for, 17
    negotiations in, 210–211
  dream team at
    information from, 53
    knowledge of, 99–100
    name selection, 40
    need for, 39
    role of, 40–41
    strategic alliances of, 62–63
    trust building by, 43–44
  foundations of, 209
  golden hammer of, 75
  listening by, 74–75
  marketing by, 28
  networking by, 56–57
  open houses by, 126
  ranking of, 9
  research by, 198
  role models for, 19–22
  talents of, xi–xii
  treatment of buyers by, 93–94
  twenty questions for sellers, 76–80
  use of technology by, 66–68
Angelou, Maya, 113
Anger
  body language of, 180–181
  controlling, techniques for, 178–179
  focus of, 180
  in negotiations, 177–179
  weakness of, 178

Anxious negotiators, 180
Appearance, 33, 36
Architectural Digest, 66
Attention spans, 74
Attitudes, 37

B

Backyards, 77
BANTA
  for buyers, 167
  for curve balls, 154
  need for, 148
  for walk-aways, 192
Bar code technologies, 121
Barkley, Charles, 40
Bathrooms, 77–78
Bel-Air, 117
Belfort, Jordan, 49
Best and final offers, 150–151
Beverly Hills, 57
  branding efforts in, 69–70
  sales challenges of, 6
  wealth of, 70
Beverly Hills Hotel, 16
Bidding wars, 166–168
Bird Street neighborhood, 34, 54
Bird, Larry, 40
Body Language, 180–181
Boston Red Sox, xix
Boundaries, 166
Brady, Tom, xiv
Branding
  mindset for, 69–70
  with press, 66–68
  by selling, 65–66
  with social media, 66–68
  through speaking engagements,
    68–69

BRAVO
    audition call from, 25–26
    success on, 66
    wedding planning on, 107
Brokers' caravans
    benefit of, 61
    networking at, 62–63
    purpose of, 68
    tactics for, 68–69
    timing of, 126–127
Brooklyn, 54
Building codes, 83
"Bumpback" clause, 155
Business styles
    assertive, 171–172
    human nature and, 174–176
    types of, 172–174
Buyers
    analyzing, 105–106
    contact info from, 61
    curve balls in, 154–155
    emotional appeals by, 149
    fears of, 106–107
    Internet use by, 120
    negative feedback from, 136
    neighborhood peer influence on, 159
    offers by
        agent-to-agent consultations in,
            144–145
        best and final, 150–151
        complexity of, 143–144
        contingency demands, 149–152
        emotions, 146
        goals, 145–146
        sweeteners in, 152–153
    open houses for, 126–127
    personalities of, 104–105
    questions for, 94–95
    relationship to, 103–104
    serious, 60
Buyers agreement, 55
Buzz, generating, 48

C
Carrying costs, 84
Cash vs. financing, 152
Catering, 128
Chandler, Dorothy, 69

Charities, 56–57
Cialdini, Robert, 58, 71
Clients
    communication modes, 79–80
    eye contact with, 37
    finding, 52
    flustered, 100
    Hollywood, 10–11
    impressing, 37–38
    instilling confidence in, 9–10
    multiple, 199–200
    potential, 33–34
    price-drop pitch to, 135–136
    questions for, 76–80
    relationship with, 4–5,
        139–140
    understanding, 34
Closes, 15
    basis of, 209–211
    commonality of, 31–32
    date for, 153
    failure of, reasons for, 32
    images for, 121
    importance of, 25
    from listing, 47–48
    reputation from, 42
    resolution of, 49
    right angle, 35
    role models for, 19
    scripts for, 15
    sense urgency in, 14
    systems for, 14–15
    technique, xv
Closing costs, 153
Code of Hammurabi, 57
Cognitive bias, 34
Collaborator (I Win – You
        Win), 173
Color photography, 117
Commissions, 155, 210–211
Commuting, 95
Compliments, 37
Compromise, xiv
Concessions, 182, 183
Concierge services, 70–71
Connecticut Muffin, 54
Contingencies, 149–152
Conveyances, 153

Counteroffers, 168–169
Creative Artists Agency (CAA), 23–24, 41
Curb appeal
    cost of, 117
    importance of, 122
    landscaping for, 78
Cutthroat compromise, xix

D
Damon, Matt, 24, 54
David, Larry, 164
Days on the market (DOM), 109–110,
    147
De Niro, Robert, 5–6
De' Medici, Cosimo di Giovanni,
    26–27
Deals
    difficulty of, 15–16
    failed, reviving, 207–208
    privacy of, 197–198
    rebuilding, 190–191
    unexpected, 201–202
Decision making
    advising on, 158
    basis of, 34
    shaping of, 58
    system thinking for, 107
Demands, extreme, 182
Democrat (I Win – You Win), 173
DiCaprio, Leonardo, 46–47
Down payments, 152–153
Draft, catching, 35–36
Drake, 56
Dream team, *see also* Altman Brothers
    information from, 53
    knowledge of, 99–100
    need for, 39
    role of, 40–41
    strategic alliances of, 62–63
    trust building by, 43
Dress style, 36
"Due diligence," 153
Dylan, Bob, 113–114

E
Earnest money deposit (EMD)
    as deal sweetener, 152
    in negotiations, 175
    requirement of, 149–150
    size of, 158
Einstein, Albert, 28
Eisenhower, Dwight D., 69
Emotional intelligence, 181–182
Emotions
    minimizing, 107, 203
    negative, 185, 188
    playing on, 116, 140
    positive, 181, 188
    powering through, 184–185
    predictable, 184
    sorting out, 7
    specific, impact of, 179
Escalator clauses, 150
Escrows, 152–153
Ewing, Patrick, 40
Exclusive right to sell, 91
Experience, organization of, 50
Extreme demands, 182
Eye contact, 37

F
Facebook, 67, 68
Feedback, 86–87, 136
Ferrari Dino, 1
Fight or flight mode, 179–180
Financing, 95, 152
Fight or flight mode, 179–180
Financing, 95, 152
First impressions
    decision making and, 34
    in Hollywood, 33–34
    opinions formed from, 32–33
    rules for, 35–38
        acting the part, 36
        complimenting, 36
        draft catching, 35–36
        dressing part, 36
        eye contact, 37
        jargon avoidance in, 35
        listening, 35
        positive attitudes, 37
Fisher, Roger, 50
Flagg, Josh, 26
Flipping properties, 10, 146
Follow-through, 17

FOMO, 158–159
Ford, Henry, 28
Franklin, Benjamin, 107
Friction, creation of, 168
Furniture, staging, 122–123

G

Game-time mentality, 10
  application of, 15
  description of, 6–8
  knowledge and, 99
  life-style selling and, 70–71
  steps, 13–14
  strategic alliances in, 62–63
Gates, Bill, 172
Gentrification, 53–54
Get-the-listing moment, 45–46
Getting to Yes (Fisher, Ury), 50
Getty, J. Paul, 69
GOAT (greatest-of-all-time), 27, xiv
Golden hammer
  anger as, 177–179
  confidence and, 184–185
  function of, 75
  for leverage, 165–168
  for price drops, 136
Google
  business page, 68
  ranking on, 67
  rankings, 121
  in Venice Beach, 54
Governing magazine, 53
Gretzky, Wayne, 12
The Guardian, 78–79

H

Hancock Park, 69
Hard-baller moves, 177–179
Harvard University, 179
Hathaway, Anne, 54
Herjavec, Robert, xii
Hollywood
  being, 169
  definition of, xiii
  game time in, 8
  making deals in, 15–16
  market of, 10–11
  virtual reality in, 119

Hollywood Hills
  Bird Street neighborhood in, 34, 54
  description of, 12
  Moroccan-style listing in, 114
Homes. *See also* Listings
  architectural styles, 130
  assessment of, 107
  deals on, 53
  depreciation of, 133
  inspection of, 149–152
  landscaping around, 112, 164
  living styles, 77–78
  new construction, 12
  overpaying for, 146
  personalization of, 111
  size, 96
  symbolism of, 31–32
  updating, 82
Honesty, 181
House of Medici, 26
Huffers, puffers and liars, 183
Human nature, 175
Humor, 191

I

I Love You, Man (film), 60
I Sell the Dream (Drake), 56
Ideas, organization of, 50
Information, power of, 57
Inspections, 149–152
Instagram, 67, 68
Intellectual (I Win – You Lose), 173
Interior design, 115–118
Internet, 67–68
It's Your Move (Altman), xiii–xiv

J

Jargon, 35
Jay-Z, 114
Jobs, Steve, 27, 172
Johnson, Lyndon B., 69
Johnson, Magic, 40
Jordan, Michael, 26, 40

K

Kahneman, Daniel, 34, 107
Kardashian West, Kim, 48

Kennedy School of Government, 179, 180
Kennedy, John F., 69
Kitchens, 77, 78
Knowledge, 97, 168

L
La Jolla beach property, 201–202
Landscape architects, 112
Landscaping, 77, 164
Leverage, 165–168
Life-style sales, 70–71
Listening
    close and, 47–48
    first impressions and, 35
    generating energy around, 48–49
    getting, 45–46
    multiple clients for, 199–200
    during negotiations, 73–76
Listing agreements, 110
Listings, 91. *See also* Homes; Properties
    average sale time, 13
    landing, tips for, 89–91
    prices, 134–137
    pricing, 84–87
    strategy for, 110–111
    unique properties, 203–205
    work phase of, 46–49
Los Angeles. *See also* individual communities of
    changing landscape of, 53–54
    film industry in, 45–50, 56
    first impressions in, 33
    Hancock Park, 69
    people investing in, 51–52
    Rams move to, 55
    sales, average time for, 13
Los Angeles Dodgers, xix
Love the Way We Used to or Better (Altman), 21

M
Malibu, 117
Malone, Kevin, 40
Manhattan Beach, 57
Marketing
    budgets, 90, 121, 128
    by generating buzz, 48, 61
    in price drop schedule, 136
    staging and, 111
    strategy for, 28, 111
Markets
    Hollywood, 10–11
    offer size and, 147–148
    pricing and, 134
    rental, 146–147
    sellers', 10–11, 150
    super-hot, 86
    supper aggressive, 107
Markkula, Mike, 27
McNabb, Donovan, 13
Microsoft, 74
Million Dollar Listing: Los Angeles, 161
    closes on, 176
        auditing for, 47–48
        being cast on, 25–26
        broker's caravan on, 129
        growing popularity of, 29
        impact of, 29
        multiple offers on, 161
        role on, 28–29
    description of, 5
    drama on, 15
Moment-to-moment lease, 55
Morrison, Jim, 54
Mortgages, 154–155
Mr. Nonchalant (I Win – You Win), 173–174
Multiple offers
    leveraging, 162–169
    in bidding wars, 166–168
    counteroffers, 168–169
    overview of, 161–162
    Pacific Palisades offer, 163–164
"My hands are tied" move, 182–183

N
Narcissism, 35
National Basketball Association (NBA), 40
National Football League (NFL), 55
Negative attitudes, 37
Negative attitude, 37
Negotiations, 24–25
    anger in, 177–179
    beginning of, 50

Negotiations *(continued)*
  confidence in, 184–185
  for counteroffers, 168–169
  difficulty of, 16
  emotional intelligence for, 181–182
  fight or flight mode in, 179–180
  hard-baller moves in, 182–183
  information for, 73–76
  for multiple offers, 162–168
  for price, 144–149
Neighborhoods, 77, 95
  agents' knowledge of, 97
  gentrification of, 53–54
  influence on buyers, 159
  knowledge of, 52–55
  open houses and, 129–130
Networking, 56–58
Nixon, Richard M., 69
Non-disclosure agreements (NDAs), 48

O
Offers. *See also* Multiple offers
  by buyers
  best and final, 150–151
  complexity of, 143–144
  contingency demands, 149–152
  curve balls in, 154–155
  market factors, 147–148
  multiple choices, 148
  sweeteners in, 152
  to sellers, 157–159
OG "old gangster" (I Win – You Lose),
    174
Open houses, 24–25, 140. *See also*
    Brokers' caravans
  brokers', 61–62, 68–70
  for buyers, 126–127
  focus of, 130–131
  getting contact info at, 61
  insiders, 62–63
  neighborhood considerations,
    129–130
  selling at, 59–60, 125–126
  stacking of, 159
Open, Work, Close mantra, 50
Opens, 15, 37, 51, 91
  definition of, 45

  diversity of, 51–52
  insider, 62–63
  launch and, 17
  navigating, 55–56
  networking at, 56–57
  pricing and, 86
  promotion of, 66
  sitting, 24
Over-ask tactic, 167, 168

P
Pacific Palisades, 151, 163–164
Parameters, 166
Parent (I Win – You Win), 173
Park Slope, Brooklyn, 54
Passive-Aggressive (I Lose – You Lose),
    172–173
Peers, neighborhood of, 159
Permits, 83
Personality types, 104–105
Photographs, 66–68, 117–120. *See also*
    Videos
Plan B. *See* BANTA
Pocket listings, 11, 134
Poseurs, 36
Prairie-style house, 131
Pricing
  basis of, 84–87
  for buyers, 94–95
  fantasy, 133–135
  markets and, 134
  negotiations, 144–149
  at opens, 86
  questions about, 79
"Proof of funds" letter, 152
Properties. *See also* Homes
  assessment of, 81–83
  description of, 113–115
  inspectors, 149–150
  interior design for, 115–116
  investment, 146
  repairs, 111–112
  suburban, 120–121
  unique, 203–205
Prospect theory, 34
Psychological drivers, 34
Punctuality, 3–4

Q

Quality-of-life questions, 79

R

Rain Man of LA Real Estate talking, 175–176
Real estate agents
    assertive, 171–172
    commissions, 155, 210–211
    community changes and, 53
    continuing learning by, 62
    faking by, 36
    first impression of, 32–34
    flustered, 100
    gossip among, 175
    honesty of by, 181, 183
    listing judgments by, 86–87
    as middle men, 57
    open houses for, 68–69, 126–129
    roles of, 6
    type-A, 41
    winning by, 5–6
    younger, 145
Reciprocity, 58
Redfin, 67, 120, 129, 134
Relaunch, 11
Rental market, 146–147
Reputations, 38
Restoration Hardware, 16
Riding the draft, 35–36
Rivera Golf Course, 163–164
A River Runs Through It feel, 120
Robinson, David, 40
Rockwell, Norman, 120
Rounders (film), 24
Rolls-Royce, 129
Royals (I Win – You Lose), 172
Rural ambiance, 120
Ruth, Babe, 26

S

Sales
    average time for, 13
    battle plan for, 109–110
    fundamental rule of, 21
    life-style, 70–71

    at open house, 125–126, 130–131
    timing of, 79
    work phase of, 46–49
Sam Adams lager incident, 20–21
San Diego, 53
Sandler, Adam, 164
Schools, 96
Scorcese, Martin, 5–6, 46
Search engine optimization (SEC), 67–68
Security systems, 78
Segal, Jason, 60
Self-defenders (You Win Some – You Lose Some), 172
Sellers
    emotional appeals to, 149
    markets, 10, 53
    motivated, 82
    offers to, 157–159
    overpricing by, 133–134
    potential, 89–90
    uncommunicative, 154
Seventy-two hour rule, 157–158
Shark Tank, xi–xii, 167
Silver Lake, 55
Slow concessions, 182
Social media, 66–68, 120
Society for Personal and Social Psychology, 33
Solidarity, 43
Speaking engagements, 68–69
Speed-dating study, 33
St. Louis Rams, 55
Staging
    benefits of, 116
    brokers' caravans, 128–129
    companies for, 116–118
    costs of, 116, 121–122
    furniture used for, 122–123
    photographing, 117–118
    power of, 118
Stahl House, 131
Starbucks, 57
Stockton, John, 40
Strategic alliance game, 62–63
Success, xiv–xv
    building on, 41–42
    dressing for, 36

Success (*continued*)
   image of, 66
   marketing and, 28
   milestones, 47
   team efforts for, 17
Super-hot markets, 86
Syracuse University, 13

T
"Take it or leave it" move, 183
Technology
   Altman Brothers use of, 66–68
   cutting edge, 66
   idea of, 27
   for tracking, 121
Thinking systems, 34, 107
Thinking, Fast and Slow (Kahneman), 34
Time
   for average sale, 13
   demands of, 10–11
   leveraging, 166
   as selling trigger, 159
   spent in house, 78
Token concessions, 167
Trulia, 67, 129
Trust building, 42–43
Twitter, 67
Type-A personality, 41
Tyson, Mike, 164

U
Underpricing, 86
University of Colorado, 13, 20
University of Syracuse, 13
Upgrades, 57
Ury, William, 50
Utilities, 83

V
Venice Beach, 54

Videos. *See also* Photographs
   over-produced, 128–129
   and stills combo, 67
   360-degree, 66
   trend toward, 121
Vimeo, 121
Volunteering, 56

W
Wahlberg, Mark, 56
Walk-away number, 162
Walk-aways
approaches to, 190–192
benefits of, 192
   contemplation of, 190
   humor use in, 191–192
points of no return in, 189–190
reason for, 187–188
Walk-throughs, 76–80, 122
Ward, Heinz, 37
West LA, 23–24
West, Kanye, 48
"We sell the dream" branding, 67
Williams, Michelle, 54
Win-win negotiations, 167
Windsor Square, 69
Wolf analogy, 46–47
The Wolf of Wall Street (film),
      46–47, 49
Work phase, 47–49
World Cup, 55
Wounded Warrior Project, 56

Y
YouTube, 68

Z
Zillow, 67–68, 129
   photo analysis by, 117, 129
   traffic on, 67–68